ILLUSTRATION &
DRAWING
STYLES & TECHNIQUES

Terry R. Presnall

Marlina Dietrich (Cat) with Plant
and Mister
#0 technical pen, drawn on
Charrette concept #900 with
waterproof India ink

NORTH LIGHT BOOKS

Cincinnati, Ohio

Illustration & Drawing: Styles & Techniques. Copyright © 1987 by Terry R. Presnall. Printed and bound in the United States of America. All rights reserved. No part of this book may be reproduced in any form or by any electronic or mechanical means including information storage and retrieval systems without permission in writing from the publisher, except by a reviewer, who may quote brief passages in a review. Published by North Light Books, an imprint of F&W Publications, Inc., 1507 Dana Avenue, Cincinnati, Ohio 45207. First edition.

Library of Congress Cataloging-in-Publication Data

Presnall, Terry R., 1948-
  Illustration & drawing.
  Includes index.
  1. Drawing—Technique.   I. Title.   II. Title: Illustration and drawing.
NC730.P74   1987   751.4   87-7801
ISBN 0-89134-193-5

Edited by Diana Martin.
Designed by Carole Winters.

To my family and friends
who made the dream
of this book come true.

CONTENTS

PART THREE

Styles
124

Introduction

This book is designed to expand your creative horizons in drawing and illustration. We live in a visual world, and it's important for artists in all stages, from the basic level to more accomplished artists, to know about the possibilities and limitations of the art mediums they are using, and the different visual effects or results that can be achieved by applying these art mediums in different ways and combinations.

This book serves as your guide to art *mediums*, how-to procedures in the *techniques* or applications of the mediums, and ways to achieve many different visual looks or *styles* in your drawings and illustrations. For that reason the book is structured in three parts: Mediums, Techniques, and Styles. Mediums are used to create the art, everything from paper and pencil, spray paint, graphite or charcoal dust, to ballpoint pens. We'll be covering both wet and dry art mediums used to create black-and-white art. Many of the techniques can successfully be rendered in color should you so desire, but I've stuck to black and white to help build your skills, knowledge, and artistic confidence.

Throughout the book you'll see the terms *techniques* and *styles* used constantly. Some artists may say a technique is the same as a style, but for our purposes, *technique* refers to the process or manner in which the art medium is applied to the paper or board, while *style* is used to describe the visual end result of the combination of medium and technique.

Whether you're an accomplished artist or a tenderfoot, you'll find your drawing knowledge, skill, and confidence will greatly improve as you experiment and try out the ideas in this book. Consider it a springboard for experimentation; it represents many experiments and art medium combinations and concoctions I've tried. You aren't obligated to try anything out of the ordinary in the application of an art medium, but I hope this book will inspire you to continually explore and experiment with different ways of creating art.

Waiting for High Tide
#1 technical pen and waterproof India ink. Dry wash done with Ebony pencil. Drawn on Pentalic Paper for Pens

MEDIUMS

Throughout Part One we will be discussing the different mediums artists use to make a mark, as well as the different types of paper best suited to each medium. In most cases, a tool is needed to aid in the medium's application and descriptions of some tools are also included.

To familiarize yourself even more with the hundreds of different art mediums and tools, I suggest you obtain an art supply catalog. This will not only describe the item but will allow you to compare the prices of individual retailers. Contact art stores and art suppliers in your area; in most cases they'll give you their catalog free of charge.

Realize that you'll probably have good days and bad days. Yesterday you drew successfully for hours on end; today you can't draw a straight line. In producing art for a living, I find that having a good day is one of the hardest things to control. On my bad days my drawings lack natural freedom—and that's something that can't be forced or faked, because if the artist is struggling, the drawing will show it. Clearing your mind is important, the mood will sooner or later pass, and getting outrageously frazzled or frustrated just isn't worth it.

Experiment and try new things with your artwork; look at familiar mediums and paper surfaces in new ways. And by all means, have fun.

Patriot Sonneteer, Selling His Wares in the Common
Crow quill and waterproof India ink, drawn on 2 ply, plate-finish bristol board.

Drawing Paper

Smooth: Graphite on Pentalic Paper for Pens

Medium: Graphite on Strathmore Series 300

Rough: Charcoal Pencil on Watercolor Paper

Your choice of support, or paper surface, plays an important role in the final look of your artwork. Above you see details from three illustrations in this book; the details show how the paper's tooth, or lack of tooth, worked with my mediums to create different textures.

The paper surface is the foundation of your artwork, the support on which the medium—charcoal, graphite, or ink—leaves its mark. Surface texture can have great impact on the overall look of a drawing; thus paper can be used as a creative element in designing your illustration. Many types of paper are manufactured to serve many different purposes. Often certain mediums work best with specific types of paper. Sometimes paper can make the difference between a successful and a so-so illustration, so it's important to choose the best paper for the job.

A paper's texture is often referred to as its *tooth*. Texture is created by the manufacturer in one of two ways: either by the paper's contents, such as wood, cotton, rag, or even fiberglass (which is added to reduce wrinkling), or by pressing it between huge steel rollers capable of creating different finishes, such as plate, pebble, tweed, linen, laid, coquille, etc.

Drawing paper is classified as either *rough, medium,* or *smooth* grade. Smooth paper is, at times, difficult to draw on since the paper lacks the bite you need for the medium to adhere to the paper's surface. On the other hand, when you use charcoal, graphite, or ink on rough paper, it skims across the raised texture of the paper rather than contacting the full surface. This paper is mainly used by watercolorists.

Hot-press paper is very smooth, with a hard, slick or "plate" surface. This paper works well along with both wet (ink) and dry (graphite, charcoal, etc.) art mediums to produce crisp, clean, accurate lines because of the paper's "hard," smooth finish. The wet medium has a tendency to dry on the surface rather than sink into the paper, which produces a more fuzzy line. (On a medium-grade, or cold-press, paper, you would have a rough time trying to produce such an accurate line because of the paper's slight tooth or fine texture.) Some examples of hot-press papers are plate-finish bristol board, plate-finish illustration board, and calligraphy papers.

Cold-press paper is slightly textured, and has a slight tooth to the surface. This paper will accommodate all art mediums, both wet and dry. About the only thing a cold-press paper or board won't do as well as its hot-press equivalent is produce the crisp, clean, accurate ink line, because of the texture of cold-press paper. Because of this slight, medium-grade characteristic, the adhesive qualities of art mediums are slightly better with cold-press rather than with hot-press paper. Some examples of cold-press papers good for dry mediums are newsprint, vellum-finished bristol board, charcoal papers, bond, and Ad Art. (Ad Art is the brand name for a brilliant white, lightweight, 100 percent rag content layout and visualizing paper. It has an excellent tooth for all dry mediums and markers, and is available in two finishes: rough and smooth.) For washes and wet mediums, all types of watercolor paper and a medium surface illustration board work well.

Watercolor paper is made of 100 percent rag fiber, so I think it's safe to say that the ink medium dries not only on the paper surface but also below the surface, in the fibers, which act like a very thin sponge. Because watercolor paper has the tendency to soak up the ink—or at least the water

I think the most trusty and versatile paper surface is plate-finish bristol board. This paper's surface can be used for, and will accept, virtually all types of mediums and techniques from wet washes, drawing inks, graphite, and charcoal to mono or lino prints.

When I draw on location, I always carry a good supply of different types of sheet paper and as a rule, the first type I'll reach for is the plate-finish bristol board. As this drawing shows, the smooth bristol board accepts the ballpoint pen ink nicely; it allows and actually helps the ballpoint line to be smooth and fluid.

First-Pic, Selling Tomatoes at the Boston Hay Market
Black Paper Mate, medium point, ballpoint pen on 2 ply plate-finish bristol board

mixed with the ink—ink washes can be applied very quickly. The rate of drying time depends on the amount of water (and/or ink medium) applied, the thickness of the paper and humidity in the air. Once watercolor paper has reached its saturation point, the drying time can be painstakingly slow, but saturating the paper can sometimes be beneficial because it allows you to bleed tones, or mold and control the tone values. If

the tone is too dark, you can blot it up with a tissue, and a lighter tone can then be reapplied.

You can buy drawing paper in a range of colors, but I find white and soft neutral-colored papers are best for drawing and illustration. Darker-colored papers, in particular, are undesirable, as they tend to subdue your drawing. What we call secondary white papers actually come in a variety of "whites." There are blue-whites

and yellow-whites. Smooth bond papers tend to be blue-white, whereas medium-grade papers, such as those used for sketching, are yellow-white. Rough papers are also yellow-white. Bristol board is available in several weights (plies) and comes in a variety of subtle pastels. Bristols tend to be bluer, which may actually make them "brighter." There is little difference between any drawing paper and the illustration board surfaces—both sur-

Fixative

You always begin your drawing on paper, and if you choose to work with charcoal, graphite, pastel, Conté, or chalk, you'll finish up by applying fixative. By doing this, you protect the work from being smudged or dirtied, and the medium won't rub off where touched. One or two light coats of fixative is sufficient. Be careful not to soak your drawing, and allow plenty of drying time between coats.

There are two types of fixative: workable and permanent. Use workable fixative to protect your drawing as you work. This type of fixative has a matte or nongloss finish that allows you to continue working on the drawing, periodically lightly spraying it to prevent smudging.

Permanent fixative is a waterproof, quick-drying, glossy fix that "seals" the drawing and should *only* be used as a final fix when the drawing is completely finished. Graphite, Conté, charcoal, chalk, or pastels won't stick to a surface that's been sprayed with a permanent fixative. I find that a medium-light coating of workable fixative works fine for the final fix of a drawing. I don't use a special can of permanent fixative for the final coat, and to me, it's an unnecessary item to buy.

faces may be identical. The only difference, call it an advantage if you wish, between the two is strength: Illustration board is strong and heavy; it can stand much abuse. I use both equally well for the same purposes with only one variation. Since I may be carrying as many as three portfolios at one time, I won't do a portfolio sample on illustration or drawing board because of its weight and thickness. I could only get half as many samples in a portfolio if I used the board, and believe me, the portfolios are already as big as they are heavy. If I used board, I'd need an extra truck to haul them around, and I'd spend most of my time stopping traffic in Boston, saying, "Back it up here, Tony."

Paper brand names may differ in different regions of the country, but the papers of the bigger paper manufacturers, like Strathmore, Arches, Aquabee, and Bienfang, are universally available. Their covers will usually designate the paper number, texture, and purpose, such as watercolor, sketching, tracing, or charcoal. The number following the manufacturer's brand name designates the different paper types and also helps the retailer when ordering different papers. For example, in the Strathmore line, the series 300 paper is a pad especially designed for student use and comes in drawing, charcoal, sketch, and watercolor surfaces. Strathmore series 400 comes in a sketch pad only, and a better grade, series 400, comes in pad and roll form. Series 500 comes in both charcoal and drawing pads of 100 percent cotton fiber paper.

Different artists demand different things from their papers and mediums, so obviously I can't give you a list of the different types of paper *you* should buy. The best way to find that out is to ask. Go to your art supply store and ask a knowledgeable salesperson what types of papers are available. Explain that you like to work in ink, for instance, and ask what two or three different papers they suggest you try. If you're the shy type or want a few opinions, call several art stores and ask salespeople what they think. Some papers are so expensive, it's like seeing a doctor, you may want a "second opinion."

As I've said, paper is important because its texture will accept certain mediums better than others. For example, a cold-press or medium-surface paper (or board) will readily accept the charcoal pencil line because its surface grabs and holds the deposited charcoal. Personally, I use all kinds of paper with all kinds of mediums. In this book you'll find examples of charcoal pencil drawings on cold-press *and* hot-press papers. Paper may not even affect your drawing—washes, acrylics, and other wet mediums work well on both smooth and textured papers, with no visual difference in texture. You won't notice the subtle texture of a graphite or charcoal line on a medium or vellum, cold-press paper or board; rough watercolor paper, however, will accentuate the charcoal line (see "Portrait of Betty," page 24).

I often break the rules, and so should you. As you experiment with different papers, notice the difference in your lines. Be adventurous—try every conceivable type of paper, from the side of a grocery bag to a piece of smooth bristol board.

The Strathmore series 400 paper used for this illustration is basically smooth with only a slight tooth. The tooth created only a slight drag on my pencil and let the charcoal adhere nicely. The tooth enhanced the scumbled line very subtly. The heavily scumbled areas create visual resting points; the eye is almost automatically drawn to these areas. (The scumbling technique will be covered in Part Two, page 56.) The "drawn" lines (which were also scumbled, by the way) are used primarily to connect the darker, more detailed areas. By working on a vertical easel I kept complete control over the scumbling.

I used workable fixative several different times on this illustration, not that I couldn't have managed without it, but having it sure helps. I first used the fixative several times in helping with the physical drawing of the picture, and then as the final step to help keep all of the medium on the paper and to protect the drawing from anything rubbing on or off. If you analyze the drawing, you'll realize your eye is first drawn to the man's face—the darkest and most detailed area. The downward movement in the connecting line of the arm guides the eye softly along the forearm into the hand and back up into the dark scumbled area between the hand and the guitar. The eye has a tendency to rest here for a moment before following the line of the guitar up to the other hand on the neck of the guitar.

Careful placement of the dark, scumbled areas helped make the illustration's V-shaped design successful. This is also a prime example of knowing when to stop in a drawing—just enough is said visually, and all the unimportant background detail is left out.

Old Man with Guitar
Berol charcoal pencil, soft, scumbled on Strathmore series 400 paper

Graphite Pencil

This illustration is a quick sketch. There is no specific style, other than just fast, loose, quick sketching and scumbling (covered on page 56) with the pencil in the course of taking visual notes. Anyone who's tried to sketch a cat knows that capturing the line is a challenge to do in a severely limited amount of time. Along with speed and simplicity in line, large negative space areas are a must when sketching.

Marlo
Graphite "2B" lead drawn on gray bond paper

The term "lead" pencil is actually a misnomer, since this common pencil doesn't contain any lead at all. The main ingredient is graphite, which is mixed with clay and then baked. The degree of hardness or softness of the graphite pencil is determined by the amount of clay added. The more clay, the harder the point; the harder the point, the lighter its color. The opposite of course is true for soft points.

Hard leads are measured by the letter "H," with a range that goes from H to 8H, the hardest. Hard lead pencils produce a grayed line quality appropriate for technical uses such as architectural drawings or engineering plans. Hard leads hold their point much longer than softer ones, and smudging is minimal. But the hard pencil lead will not produce a dark line even with a great pressure force; more than likely, the lead will snap off. Another disadvantage of using the hard lead pencil to sketch with is that if you bear down with a lot of force trying to achieve a darker area or tone, you could severely score the paper. Then if you find you've made a mistake or want to rework that area of the drawing and manage to erase the hard lead graphite tone, you're still stuck with the scored paper area. Trying to redraw over that area will be impossible or produce an undesirable area in your drawing.

Soft leads are measured by the letter "B" and range from B to 8B, the softest. Soft leads are darker in color than hard ones because they contain larger amounts of graphite. For sketching, I always reach for a soft pencil because soft lead gives a rich, dark line. Values are easily controlled with pencil pressure. Lighter tones can be produced with lighter pressure,

darker tones with more pressure.

Some pencil manufacturers may use a number system for the pencil rating of No. 1 (which is always the softest), No. 2, No. 3 and No. 4. You have seen such a rating on the most common writing pencil, the No. 2, which is popular because of its dark, medium-soft lead. Little pressure is needed to produce a legible line, which means the writer can write a longer time without tiring, and the pencil will hold its point much longer than a very soft pencil.

The wooden barrel of a typical sketching or writing pencil is round or hexagonal. Cedar is most frequently used for the barrel on high-quality pencils.

To stretch the life of a pencil, buy a pencil lengthener, which is made up of an aluminum shaft and a wooden body. The lengthener will hold any pencil remnant with either a round or hexagonal barrel shape, so you can continue to use the pencil even after it's too small to hold in your hand.

Mechanical Pencil

Mechanical pencils have lots of advantages. The body length of the mechanical pencil will never change because you never have to sharpen it. The lead and the lead point can be retracted into the pencil for safe carrying. A variety of lead hardnesses can be used with the same pencil body and can be easily and quickly changed. You may wish to first start your drawing with an "HB" or a "B" lead and change to a "BBB" lead for the tones, or vice versa. Different barrel diameters and body grips are available. Since these barrel widths and grips vary widely, it's worth a

This sketch was done in a hurry, almost a frenzy. I was outside with only a few sheets of white bond paper and a mechanical pencil with a "B" lead. As I watched children throwing bread into the water, I noticed how the ducks and geese positioned themselves in the water. Aggression and hunger seemed to overrule size. This intrigued me, so first I sketched the ducks, then the goose. The water was added almost as an afterthought to keep the three birds from floating in white space, and as a means of bouncing dark and white shapes off the three birds. The feather areas are meant to be more suggestive than accurate.

Lakeside Trio
Graphite "B" lead on white bond paper

9

American Gothic
*Drawn and scumbled on a hard
surface with an Ebony pencil on
#950 Hammermill white bond
paper*

Sometimes I have many drawings and paintings in various stages of completion taped to the walls of my studio. That way they don't get beat up or lost, and I can study them off and on throughout the day. All this leads up to the story behind the drawing "American Gothic."

One day I removed a sheet of paper from my pad, only to remember something else I had to do first. I taped the new sheet on the wall next to a few half-finished drawings, and flew out the door. Hours later I returned and, passing by the hanging sketches, stopped momentarily to study them. I picked up an ebony pencil and looking at one of the half-finished sketches, began to impulsively draw my "what if it looked like this, and added that," notations on the clean sheet of paper I had hung up earlier that day.

These notations turned into an interesting drawing, reminding me of a typical elderly couple. I added the pitch fork, and that's what gave the drawing its name.

This was done with my favorite graphite medium, an Eberhard-Faber Ebony pencil. Notice here the variety of widths and types of line made by the Ebony.

Its soft, black graphite reveals something more about this drawing: The paper wasn't properly cushioned, so the hard, bumpy texture of the painted wall was picked up and shown in the scumbled graphite areas. Not that it ruined the drawing; in fact it adds a little interest to the line, but I don't think I'll do it again. Next time I'll make sure the paper is properly cushioned.

trip to your favorite art supply store to "test drive" a few of the mechanical pencils to find the type that feels best or most comfortable in your hand. If you have smaller or thinner fingers, the thinner and possibly smoother pencil barrel may be your cup of tea. I have what is known as a "butcher's" hand, with a wide palm and short, stubby, chubby fingers, and find I like the wider pencil barrels with the stronger ribbed, molded finger grips.

Drawing leads for the mechanical pencil are available in 14 degrees and several diameters, the standard .2mm (.008"), .3mm (.012"), .5mm (.020"), .7mm (.028"), .9mm (.036").

If you wish to keep a fine point at all times on a mechanical pencil lead, you can use a pencil pointer. The pencil fits in the pointer, and with a few quick circular motions of the wrist, will sharpen the point quickly and with no mess.

Ebony Pencil

The Eberhard-Faber Ebony pencil is by far my favorite for sketching and rendering final art in graphite. This pencil has the finest quality soft, jet-black graphite, which produces an extra smooth line. The graphite core is a little wider in diameter than the regular pencil. An Ebony pencil will easily render line widths from very thin to wide, and because of its extra dark, quality graphite doesn't require a lot of pressure.

Most paper surfaces will accept the Ebony pencil line, but I prefer to use a paper with a slight tooth such as a cold-press illustration board, cold-press bristols, Strathmore series 300 sketch paper, newsprint, and 100 percent rag layout papers. The tooth gives a slight drag on the pencil and seems to grip the graphite nicely, so it adheres to the paper. The tooth also can add character to the line.

Sketching with a Soft Pencil

Ideally, sketching should be a spontaneous, uninterrupted creative endeavor. The next time you spend time sketching, try this working method and see if it doesn't allow you to be more productive. Sharpen three or four pencils of the same grade—"B," "BB," or "BBB." Use a soft lead because it will give a greater variety of line thicknesses. As you sketch, and as one point wears down, continue your work by using one of the still-sharpened points for fine lines, and the now-worn points for broad lines. You'll be able to work in a continual flow rather than having to stop periodically, losing spontaneity and concentration as you waste valuable time sharpening your pencils.

Also, it's important that your drawing surface is comfortable, not too soft and not too hard. A too-soft surface may be difficult to draw on and have a spongy effect under the pencil point. If the drawing surface is too hard, the pencil will tend to deposit too much medium with very little pressure, so tone variations will be harder to control. Also, if the hard surface isn't completely smooth, any patterns, scratches, or irregularities may be accidentally picked up by the pencil line in the drawing. A single sheet of bond paper on a wooden drawing board may accidentally pick up the wood grain from the board in the drawing, for instance. Also, if you apply too much pressure on this single sheet, you may accidentally poke holes in the paper or tear through it with the pencil point.

Pad your drawing surface slightly. Slip one or two sheets of the same type of paper you are drawing on between the hard drawing surface and your sketch. This padding combined with the pressure used to apply your pencil to the paper will help the paper accept the graphite better.

The quickly scumbled graphite line in this sketch was easily accepted by the bond paper I used. The slight tooth of the paper grabs and easily holds the graphite medium. The ease with which the continual back and forth motion of the line was executed will visually testify to that. The darkness or dark tone of the sketched line was achieved by applying moderately heavy pressure and combining this with a soft "B" lead. This took only a few minutes to sketch.

Girl with Hat
Graphite "B" pencil scumbled and drawn on white bond paper

Erasers

Erasers can save a drawing sometimes. Their primary uses are to remove the artist's mistakes, to lighten tones on the paper's surface, and of course to perform general clean-up tasks, such as removing smudging or the pencil sketch lines after a drawing is rendered in ink. There are many different types of erasers on the market today, and each type has its own job to do. Some varieties are available in pencillike strips (both manual and electric), squares that wear themselves away (FaberCastell Artgum), the familiar rectangles and oblongs, pliable shapes (kneadable erasers), and paper-wrapped eraser pencils. Some are composed of stretchable formulas (kneaded rubber), nonsmearing formulas (RubKleen), one that chemically erases India ink and has a vinyl end, and even plastics and nonflammable liquids. The list goes on. I'll tell you right from the start, I haven't tried all of the different eraser types, although some sound very interesting. Fighting your way through the eraser jungle, you may find you like one type over another, and if you are happy with the type of erasers you are using, then by all means, stick with them. All of my erasing needs are taken care of by three different erasers. I prefer the kneaded rubber eraser, the pink pearl, and the electric eraser. First the kneaded rubber eraser: Pliable as putty, but not as oily, it's used both for "picking up" the medium from the paper's surface, and rubbing it off. You can form and shape a kneaded eraser for all types of erasing, from large fore- or background areas to very small, detailed facial areas. You can literally use it as a drawing tool. Smearing or smudging with a rubber eraser is minimal, and its nonabrasive, soft texture prevents damage to your paper. This eraser is good for removing graphite, charcoal, carbon, and pastels.

The second type of eraser, the pink pearl, is used mostly for "blasting" areas. Blasting simply means removing large areas or portions of the art medium (graphite, charcoal, or pastel) from the paper surface, and also those areas that have been rubbed in and are harder to remove (which the kneaded eraser cannot erase). If you need to erase large areas in a drawing, use this soft eraser to rub the surfaces; only discreet deposits of erasing debris will be left on the paper surface. If you use a gum eraser, on the other hand, most of the erasing debris will ball up and be left behind on your paper surface. Blowing hard on the paper won't remove all of this type of eraser from the paper's surface, it has to be gently rubbed off with the hand or large brush. You could easily smudge the drawing and end up with a big mess.

My third favorite is the electric eraser. This is a hand-held machine that has a convenient on-off switch on the handle. It uses standard 7" × ¼" eraser strips that can be easily changed. Eleven different eraser types can be used; these types are designated and identified by their colors, and are generally used for graphite and ink. My all purpose electric eraser is the soft, green one, which I mostly use for ink on a very hard paper surface. Erasing shields are available to use with the electric eraser and prove to be very helpful and handy. These are thin stainless steel shields with various size and shape cutout openings that allow for tight, small-area erasing. They're a must with the electric eraser.

A useful liquid "eraser" is Pro White. This is the brand name (other brands are available; the product is virtually the same) for a water-soluble, very opaque, white paint, which covers well on most surfaces such as acetate, photos, paper, etc., and may easily be diluted for wet washes with other water-soluble art mediums and combinations. It will not yellow with age. This product is a must when you are working with dark or black art mediums for touching up, cleaning up, or correcting mistakes.

Pro White

Pink Pearl Eraser

Kneaded Rubber Eraser

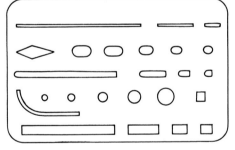

Erasing Shield

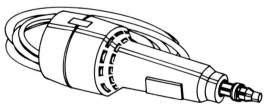

Electric Eraser

Electric Eraser Strips

13

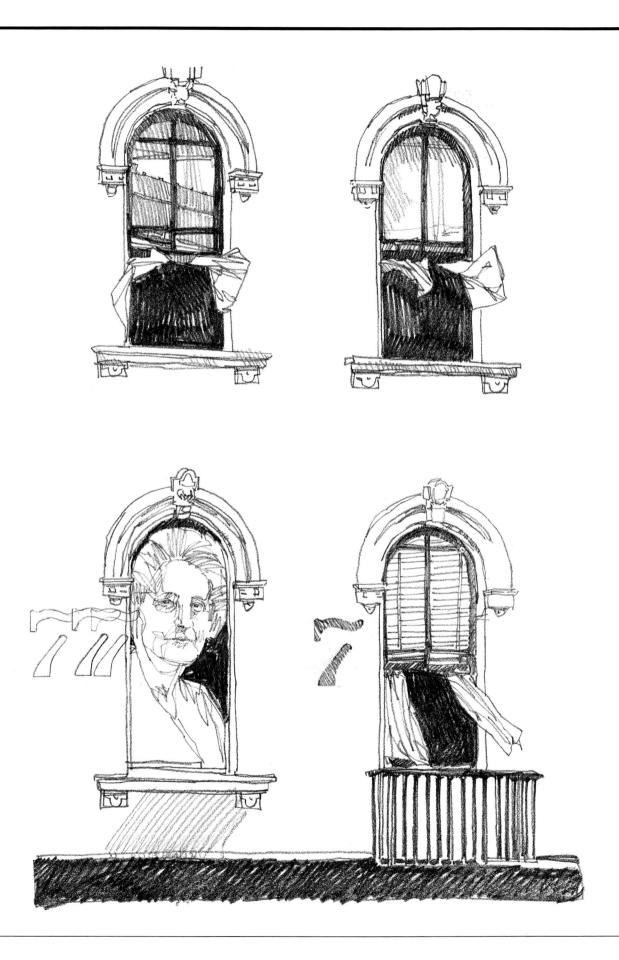

I got the idea for this drawing as I drove past a building and noticed the curtains blowing in the breeze and an elderly lady sunning herself through a third floor window. The address also grabbed my eye—a big number seven. I stopped the car and began to sketch, still sitting in the car, using what I had on hand at the time: a mechanical pencil with a "B" lead and a pad of Strathmore series 400 medium surface paper. After loosely sketching the windows, curtains, and fire escape I drove back to my studio and gave the incomplete drawing a very light coat of workable fixative to protect the graphite from smudging.

My biggest decision in finishing the drawing was whether or not to add the brick texture; because the building was made of red brick, in my mind's eye this was visually missing from the drawing. But I wasn't sure if this would make or break the clean look of the sketch. As an experiment, I covered the drawing with a large piece of tracing paper and drew in the brick, but it only seemed to clutter the drawing with unnecessary line.

Next I made a stencil of the number seven on a piece of 2 ply bristol board, traced it onto the drawing, and with the stencil still in place, filled in the number with graphite pencil. I decided to add three more outlined sevens to give the drawing a little movement.

Then, because the fire escape rail on the bottom right seemed visually a little too powerful (dark), I added the woman to balance out the bottom right. The railing pulled the eye to the edge of the page, but then the flow stopped abruptly; somehow I had to swing the eye back up into the drawing. Adding the woman and keeping the shaded areas behind her to a minimum seemed to work—the dark area inside the window leads the eye back into the drawing. Leaving the woman linear, not shading her, helps provide a route for the eye to travel: from the dark area in the window, through the woman, and into the number sevens for a visually light ending. Finally, I applied another medium coat of workable fixative.

7 South Main Street
Graphite, "B" pencil, drawn on Strathmore series 400 medium surface drawing paper

Carpenter's Pencil

A carpenter's pencil or flat sketching pencil is long and rectangular, to the point of being termed "flat." It's often referred to as a flat sketching pencil because of its unique shape: a one-eighth inch thick piece of graphite covered by one-quarter to one-half inch wide pieces of wood. This pencil is good for sketching, layouts, and lettering and is available in three degrees, "2B," "4B," and "6B."

The flat sketching pencil will give visual results almost identical to that of the graphite drawing stick; both use the edge of the tool to render line. The difference is in the way you hold a carpenter's pencil—like a pencil. It must be held in the same position relative to the paper in order to continually produce the same kind of line.

This pencil produces a very hard, even stroke. To sharpen a carpenter's pencil, use a sharp razor blade to make your initial cuts through the wood; a conventional pencil sharpener won't work here because of this tool's odd form. Practice shaping the graphite edge with a razor blade to create different line thicknesses. You can even experiment by notching the tip of the graphite for one-stroke parallel lines, such as for wooden slats on the side of a barn.

After many hours of experimenting with all types of papers, I've found those with a medium smooth surface best suited for this medium. Generally, a good quality "sketch" paper will do; a harder, smoother surface or plate-finished paper, such as bristol board, won't accept the line as well. The medium has the tendency to skate across the smoother surface, and this is evident in the line it produces. Unlike the hot-press surface, the Strathmore series 300 (cold-press) paper has a nice tooth that accepts the graphite line nicely and holds it to its surface. And, because of this characteristic, shade tones can be easily controlled.

There is also a chisel pencil which is a smaller version of the carpenter's pencil. It doesn't come with a chisel edge, but its lead can easily be shaped into a chisel edge. The chisel pencil is the same size as the common, wooden-barrel writing pencil; the only difference is the shape of the rectangular lead and the fact that it has to be sharpened by hand.

Carpenter pencil

Medium thick carpenter pencil line

Notched carpenter pencil for combined thick and thin lines

Notched carpenter pencil for two thin and one thick line

Chisel pencil

Medium thick chisel pencil line

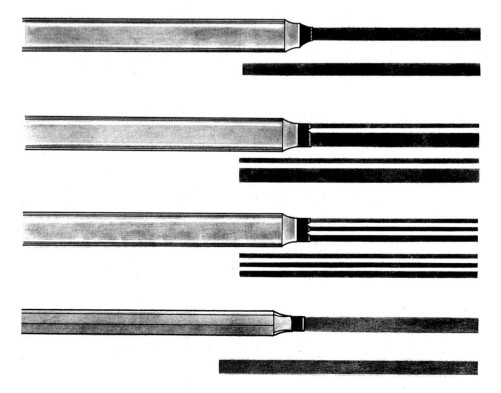

I chose a carpenter's pencil for this drawing because I thought it would help show motion. The parallel lines in the strumming arm of the guitarist help the viewer's eye to blend these lines together and create the illusion that the arm is actually moving. The cigarette smoke streams upward, flattens out, and dissipates with a simple linear motion. I used a medium-tooth paper because it accepts the graphite line better than either a smooth or rough surface.

Mississippi Blues
General's flat sketching pencil, "2B," drawn on Strathmore series 300 paper

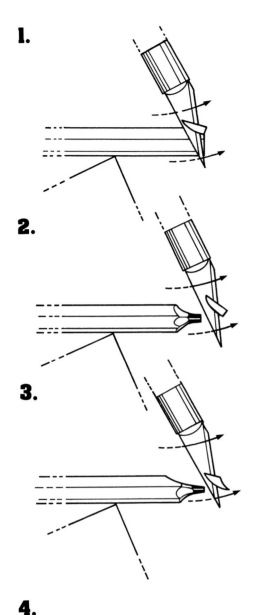

1.

2.

3.

4.

Sharpening Your Pencil by Hand

There are several reasons for learning how to sharpen your pencil by hand. The first is the high cost of art materials, which forces most artists to be as cost-effective as possible. Second, a properly sharpened point is vital to many of your drawings and illustrations.

Another reason hand sharpening should be mastered is that when you're drawing on location, probably the last thing you'll carry is a large, cumbersome crank pencil sharpener.

To do the job properly, you need either a single edge razor blade or a small, very sharp knife. If you are home, a small, very sharp, paring knife or single-edge razor blade will do just fine, but if you are drawing on location, a sharp retractable penknife would be a safer bet.

1. Place the end you want to sharpen against a firm surface. Holding the pencil firmly, cut in the direction away from your body and fingers, toward the tip of the pencil; make small slices about one-eighth- to one-quarter inch long.

2. Keep as much wood on the pencil as you can because it's vital for supporting the graphite; if too much is removed, your point may break off. And don't use excessive whittling pressure either, or you'll snap off the graphite.

3. Move one-quarter inch further down the pencil shaft and gently cut off more wood. Again take care not to break or snap off the graphite.

4. Your pencil is now ready to use or you can hone the graphite to a point using the edge of your cutting blade, fine sandpaper or scrap paper.

5. If you use sandpaper or scrap paper, move the pencil back and forth in long, even-pressured strokes while slowly turning the pencil's body.

Be careful never to remove the identification letters on your pencil; chances are you won't remember what type it was to replace it.

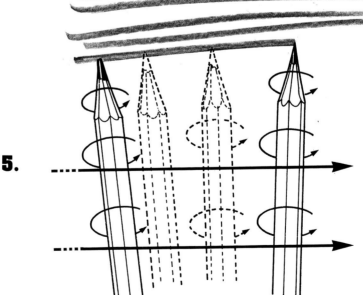

5.

Graphite Drawing Stick

Graphite drawing sticks are literally what their name implies—unprotected pieces of graphite, three inches long and one-quarter inch square. The line differs from the typical pencil line (drawn with the point of the lead) because the entire edge of the graphite stick is applied to the paper. It looks more like a wide stroke than a line. Tone values and darks are achieved by the amount of pressure applied in the stroke—the more pressure, the darker the line. Available in "2B," "4B," and "6B," graphite sticks are especially suited for layouts and sketching.

Different lengths may be made simply by breaking the graphite sticks.

The different lengths of stick will produce different widths strokes. For example, for the broader, larger areas and strokes, I will use a larger (longer) piece of graphite stick and the same applies using a smaller (shorter) piece to produce a smaller, more detailed stroke. I surely wouldn't use a 1 1/2-inch piece of drawing stick to draw the detailed parts of the face (eyes, nose, etc.). I'd change over to a smaller, 1/4-inch piece. A clean break is desirable because this makes the small piece of graphite easier to hold with the index finger and thumb tips. Remember, the smaller the piece of stick is, the harder it is to hold with the fingertips—graphite is slippery

stuff. Actually, the only drawback in using this medium is that, without the wooden barrel of a graphite pencil, the graphite gets very messy in the hand.

The best eraser to use with this medium is the kneaded rubber type, because it will pick up the soft graphite rather than smudge it. And unlike the pink pearl and gum erasers, the kneaded rubber eraser won't leave a deposit on the paper. Any eraser deposit left on the paper's surface can be disastrous, because if you accidentally draw over this deposit, you'll get a broken line.

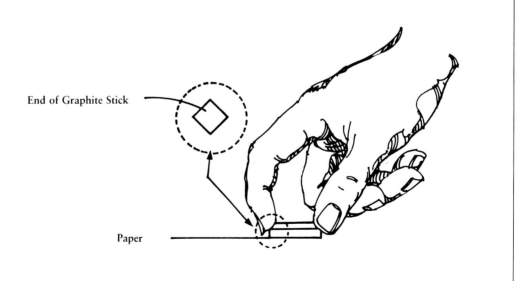

Because, unlike a pencil, the entire length or edge of a graphite stick is applied to the paper, you grasp it between the tips of your index finger and thumb. Break the sticks, which are sold in three-inch by one-quarter-inch pieces, into convenient lengths. The width of your line is determined by the length of your stick of graphite and the direction of your stroke. Remember, though, that very small pieces of graphite are slippery and hard to hold.

End of Graphite Stick

Paper

Once while I was hurrying to wear down the square end of a graphite stick into a rounder shape, I was scumbling the edge of the stick as hard as I could on a sheet of extra paper, and the graphite flew out of my hand. I picked up the stick and, holding it differently than before, made a series of horizontal strokes on a piece of scrap paper, eventually filling the entire sheet. The next day I came across this piece of scrap paper and realized that the patterns and shapes I'd randomly created could be applied to drawing technique. This is the technique I used on "Florida Landscape." The broad strokes created by the length of the graphite stick are what gives this technique a tonal look. The stroke motion follows the object's shape or contour, and tonality or shading is accomplished either by a series of linear strokes laid next to each other, or by making a broad stroke with the length of the graphite stick. Most shading should be left until last because the broader strokes used to make the shaded areas will quickly wear down the edge of the graphite stick that you'll need to produce the line.

Florida Landscape
Graphite drawing stick, "2B" Koh-I-Noor Hardtmuth, drawn on Attica pad paper

This illustration began as a portrait, showing only the head and shoulders, but luckily I started in the middle of the paper (as I generally do), because you can see how the drawing size grew and grew. To start, I selected four different lengths of graphite stick: $1/4''$, $1/2''$, $3/4''$, and $1''$. (Graphite can be broken into whatever length you need. I use longer pieces for broader strokes or larger areas, and shorter pieces for smaller, more detailed strokes.) First I did the line drawing of the face, hair, and shoulders—then the drawing continued to the bottom of the dress. Next I did the shading on the face and dress; then I drew and shaded the background. I handled the drawing and shading this way because I wanted a delicate balance between the foreground and background, so one wouldn't overwhelm the other. Finally I added the square detailing in the dress with a .5mm Pentel "Sharp" mechanical pencil, using a "B" graphite lead. Two separate, light coats of workable fixative were sprayed on as the final step in the drawing.

Sara's Silent Prayer
Graphite drawing stick, "2B" Koh-I-Noor Hardtmuth, drawn on Strathmore series 300 paper

21

These illustrations were both done with graphite drawing sticks, but for "Sisters" I used a minimum of shading, preferring to let the lines speak for themselves. Because it feels more natural, I find myself drawing mainly in vertical strokes; when a horizontal or angled line is needed I'll simply rotate the drawing itself so I can still make the vertical stroke. Pentalic Paper for Pens is extremely white and has a smooth surface especially suited for calligraphy, technical, and crow-quill pens, but I like to use it with dry mediums as well. It's great to experiment with because this hot-press or smooth paper doesn't have the ability to grab the medium and hold it. The graphite has the tendency to skate across this smoother surface, as you can see in the lines of this drawing.

Sisters
Graphite drawing stick, "2B" Koh-I-Noor Hardtmuth, drawn on Pentalic Paper for Pens

End of the Day
Graphite drawing stick, "2B"
Koh-I-Noor Hardtmuth, drawn
on Strathmore series 300 paper

For "End of the Day" I used quite a bit of shading to evoke the shadows and contrasts of evening, as well as to suggest the heavy feeling that comes after a long day of hard work. Strathmore series 300 paper is a good drawing surface to use for these effects because this cold-press paper has a tooth that accepts the graphite line nicely, and tonality can be easily controlled.

Charcoal Pencil

By carefully matching your medium to a paper, you can enhance or vary the characteristics of that particular medium. Notice how the charcoal pencil added the heavy texture of the paper to its line. Experiment with different papers to discover how best to achieve a particular illustration effect.

Portrait of Betty
Berol charcoal pencil, medium, drawn on watercolor paper

The charcoal pencil is, as the name suggests, a charcoal core encased in wood to add extra strength, and a handle. Linseed oil is usually added in manufacturing, giving charcoal its rich color and density, and the ability to adhere to paper. Charcoal pencils make soft, jet black marks and work equally well for both tone drawing and line. Light tones are as easy to make as dark tones.

The degree of hardness or softness is measured in a manner similar to graphite pencils, but different manufacturers have various ways of labeling the degrees of their charcoal pencils. With some brands, "H" is hard and "HHH" the hardest; "B" is soft and "BBB" the softest. Other manufacturers simply label charcoal as soft, medium, and hard. Try several brands and compare the manufacturers' labels with the performance of the pencils.

Charcoal pencils, like graphite, leave their mark or deposit on the paper's surface. So if the paper surface has any type of texture or tooth, the drawn line deposited on the paper's surface will affect and reflect that characteristic and will create a different *style* or look to the medium. These effects can be seen and compared by comparing the line quality of "On Vacation" (Strathmore series 400 paper) on the opposite page, and "Portrait of Betty" (Strathmore series 500 watercolor paper), left.

Charcoal pencils have a tendency to wear down fast, even with the lightest of pressure. For the harder charcoal pencils, I prefer to use a conventional, hand-crank pencil sharpener that mounts on the wall (the electric

sharpeners have a tendency to eat up the pencil faster). The hand-crank sharpener is faster than hand sharpening with a razor blade, but for the very soft charcoal pencils, the hand crank may have a tendency to snap off the extremely soft brittle tip of the pencil. Hand sharpening with a razor blade will work best for the soft types.

As with the very soft graphite pencils, when a charcoal tip wears down, it's easy to restore a sharp point. On an extra sheet of paper, roll the side of the charcoal tip using light pressure. This may take several rolling strokes to form the point on the charcoal tip, but you'll find this method saves a lot of time and greatly extends the pencil's life.

Virtually all of my erasing needs for charcoal pencils are met by using a kneaded rubber eraser. Generally, my drawn charcoal line has not been put down with such force that it will take a gum or pink pearl eraser to scrub it off the paper's surface. When I make a mistake or change my mind on a drawing, I first will dab or poke the drawn area with the kneaded eraser. This eraser, which resembles soft clay, will pick up most of the medium from the paper surface. After that, if more erasing in that spot is needed, gentle rubbing with the kneaded rubber eraser should work nicely.

Fixatives are always used to protect charcoal art, both during the working stages and on completion.

This drawing appeared as a spot illustration at about half its original size of 6½" × 9". I intentionally made the line weight quite heavy so the illustration would stand the reduction, and since the text was to wrap around the top and upper left of the woman's head, I balanced the composition accordingly. The woman and the child on her lap were drawn from a photo reference. I added the third figure for balance, and the background was drawn to tie the visual together. I chose charcoal for the drawing because of its line flexibility; charcoal provides both line thickness and line density. If you carefully study the illustration, you'll see that the most important parts— the positive areas—are mainly composed of heavier lines. The thinner lines are used only to suggest the outlined negative space areas and were purposely designed to accentuate and accommodate the positive areas.

On Vacation
"BBB" Wolff's charcoal pencil, drawn on Strathmore series 400 paper

Carbon Pencil

The carbon pencil is similar to charcoal in its drawing characteristics. It is hard and oily like charcoal and leaves a rich, black line on your paper. Like all pencils, carbon is available in various degrees of hardness; unlike graphite, which lays on top of the paper's tooth, carbon goes deeper into the tooth and doesn't smear if you try to erase it. Carbon pencil is one of the best mediums to draw with, in my opinion. Do your preliminary sketches in graphite or charcoal, then render the final art in carbon. It holds a fine point, and tonal qualities range from charcoal gray to jet black.

The key to rendering this illustration was a carbon pencil that I kept well pointed at all times. This let me control line thickness and placement, plus detailing and values. To build shapes using line mass, such as you see here, rather than outline, you should lay the lines in so they follow and fill in the contours of the objects. While this piece is mostly composed of dark, positive areas, I incorporated negative shapes as my highlight areas, such as the hat and hand.

Take One
"B" Wolff's carbon pencil, drawn on 100% rag paper

Drawing on Coquille Board

The coquille board wears its texture on its hard surface. The rough coquille board (also available in smooth, some manufacturers may list them as coarse and fine) has a "mezzotint" pattern pressed on the board surface, which means it is most compatible with mediums that are deposited on the board surface. Charcoal, graphite drawing stick, and Conté are best. The surface pattern produces a type of halftone effect and can be very interesting. I prefer to use a medium such as the broad edge of a graphite drawing stick to get the full effect of the coquille board's surface pattern. Of course, a fixative should be used on any type of medium that will smudge or smear off the board.

Note the clean, smooth line obtainable with one stroke of the graphite drawing stick and how easily the graphite shows the finely textured pattern of the rough coquille board. Minor erasing was done (to correct mistakes) with a kneaded rubber eraser, and two light coats of workable fixative were sprayed on for protection.

*Three views of Billy
Koh-I-Noor Hardtmuth "2B"
drawing sticks, drawn on rough
coquille board*

Vine Charcoal

Vine charcoal is simply a very soft, bare stick of charcoal. It's about six inches in length with three-sixteenths-inch thick rounded ends. The degrees of hardness of this medium are measured in numbers, with 1 the softest, to 4 the hardest.

Vine charcoal is made from small branches of vine or willow, which are heated and carefully burned in kilns. Its primary use other than sketching on paper is for preliminary sketches on canvas before oil painting. Because vine charcoal does not adhere strongly, it can be easily blown or brushed off after the planning stages are complete.

Personally, I have no use for vine charcoal in my work. It crumbles very easily and adheres poorly to paper. I find it difficult to control, with tonality and line quality inconsistent compared with the more refined charcoal pencil or compressed charcoal stick. A word of caution—be aware that you can scratch your paper because an area in the charcoal stick didn't turn completely into charcoal and still contains small bits of wood.

Conté Crayon

Conté is a well-known type of French "chalk." Conté is composed of graphite or pigment, clay, and water, which are mixed into a paste, baked in kilns, and then pressed into sticks. Conté is available in both stick and pencil form, in four colors: sanguine (red, with four shades available), bistre (sepia), white, and black (three grades of black are available: soft, medium, and hard). Conté gives rich tonal qualities, smooth lines, and works well on most types of paper.

Don't confuse Conté with colored pencils. Colored pencils are made of dyes and kaolin (clay). Conté contains no wax and may be difficult to entirely erase. If you need to erase large areas, you probably won't be able to remove all the Conté, and you're guaranteed to have a stained paper surface. Your best bet is to start out sketching very lightly and gradually get darker and darker as the drawing progresses. The kneaded rubber eraser works pretty well on Conté, but if you have to blast an area, pick up as much as you can with a kneaded eraser and then rub the area with a pink pearl eraser.

Using a photo as reference, I first very lightly pencil sketched in the drawing, then went over that line with Conté. Although the drawing was done on a smooth, plate-finish illustration board, some of the paper's surface texture (even though there's not supposed to be any) is seen in the black background areas. The medium black Conté line that was used in this drawing seems increasingly heavier, visually blacker, and wider when additional pressure is applied to the Conté in its application to the paper.

Marlo with Art Deco Statue
Medium black Conté crayon drawn on Charrette High-Tech plate-finish illustration board

This illustration appeared as the cover art for a brochure announcing an art show with the theme of transcending time. The illustration was printed in sepia tones.

To create "Victorian Beauty" I first completed the entire line drawing with sanguine Conté and sprayed on a light coat of workable fixative to protect the Conté line. Next I used the dry wash technique *(which is described in detail in Part Two, page 62)* by rubbing sanguine Conté on a separate sheet of paper and using a wadded piece of tissue paper to transfer this built-up deposit of Conté to the drawing, adding tones to the face, hat, and clothing. This piece of tissue paper with the medium on it enabled me to get large controlled areas of light tone as I gently applied it to the drawing. The light tone was then shaped—areas overlapping the drawn line were removed with a kneaded eraser, then sprayed with workable fixative. For darker tones, the method was repeated, building light tone upon light tone until the desired darkness was achieved. Then I applied a final light coat of workable fixative.

Victorian Beauty
Conté "3B," drawn on 2-ply, plate-finish bristol board

Ink

There are many types of ink on the market today, in just about every color imaginable. Colored drawing inks are vivid and transparent; colors can be mixed to achieve intermediate shades. A tone or shade's darkness is determined by the amount of water added to dilute the ink. The more water, the lighter the shade.

India ink is a dark black liquid available in waterproof and water-soluble formulas. The most significant difference between the two types of India ink is their permanence. Shellac gives India ink its waterproof characteristic; this type of ink is the most durable. Waterproof India ink can be thinned and used with water; the waterproof properties come into effect only after the ink has dried. Water-soluble India ink also mixes well with water for washes, but as the name implies, it isn't waterproof and is not as durable. This ink cannot be used with other water-based mediums. If you intend to use water in any form, such as washes, acrylics, or watercolors along with the ink, use waterproof India ink. (We'll discuss ink washes on page 80.)

There are also specially formulated inks on the market for use in technical pens. These waterproof and water-soluble inks have nonclogging properties and flow freely with ultradense, opaque qualities to produce continuous, controlled lines.

This illustration was taken partially from a photo I took at, naturally, a July 4th celebration. The entire illustration was done flat on the drawing board in the studio. I used "contour" shading lines with the simplified drawing and added a suggestion of crosshatch in the flag for variety and a hint of a darker tone. (Crosshatching is covered in Part Two, page 49.)

A new #0 technical nib was used with waterproof India ink, and as you can tell by looking at the fluid line it produced, it was flowing extremely well that day.

July 4th Celebration
#0 (0.35mm) Rapidograph technical pen, Pelikan Special Inks 9066, drawn on Pentalic Paper for Pens.

This drawing was done on-the-spot, while sitting down by the pond on a most enjoyable August afternoon. That day I carried a pad of 11" × 14", 2 ply plate-finish bristol board, a small bottle of waterproof India ink, a soft pencil, a kneaded eraser, and a crow quill pen. The drawing was actually put together in three stages. First, I pencil sketched the swan boat that was tied to the dock and inked in the line; then I added the paddler behind the cast iron swan (they were paddle boats) and the passengers, which was easy because it took about a half an hour to assemble and board the two dozen passengers. After the people had been penciled in and redrawn in ink, I then added the water and background, drawing the boat as if it were in the middle of the pond. The third and final stage took place in the studio, where I added the background, boat shadows and other black ink areas, using a small brush. I'll carry nothing but waterproof India ink on my outings; this allows me the flexibility and option to change my mind and rework the areas in the drawing at a different place or time. I wouldn't be able to add a wet wash or any medium pertaining to water if I had used a water-soluble India ink—

I'd then wash away the line. When completely finished, I softly erased all of the pencil sketch lines with a kneaded eraser.

I prefer and use a crow quill pen because it's flexible, will allow a fast easy-flowing line, and is fun to use. The bristol board nicely accepts the line of the crow quill nib, and the ink dries on its hard, less absorbent surface.

Swan Boat in the Boston Common
Crow quill and brush, India ink, drawn on 2 ply, plate-finish, bristol board.

Pen Point

Pen points or drawing nibs are used in both drawing and lettering. A drawing pen point, or nib, is made of steel and is flexible enough to produce a variety of line widths. These pen points are available in several shapes and sizes for different functions. The Hunt Artist Pens, #22B Extra Fine, #56 School, and #101 Imperial to name a few, are ideal for drawing, lettering, and fine line techniques.

Proper care and cleaning of your pen points will ensure their functioning for a long time. Don't allow any residue to build up on your points as this may interfere with the quality of your drawn lines. Pen points can be cleaned easily by simply rinsing them under a running faucet. Use soap and water for stubborn areas. The key point on cleaning is to remember to remove the pen point from the pen holder before cleaning, especially if the pen holder has a metal clip to hold the pen point in. If the point is not removed, the metal clip may rust and freeze up with the point inside. When a pen point and holder are cleaned, both should be thoroughly dried with a tissue or cotton cloth. (Technical pen points are a different story; cleaning a technical pen will be covered on page 42.)

When choosing your points, you'll also need to look at and feel the pen holders, which are available in different widths and lengths. Choose the thickness of holder that feels most comfortable in your hand.

"Cameo" was rendered by a Hunt "Drawing" #99, flexible, extrafine, round-pointed, steel pen. This is also a superb nib for sketching the fast, fine line, and different line widths are easily available from this nib by applying different amounts of pressure to the nib. As for the drawing, it was done rath-er large and is a portrait of a girl with her hair blowing in the breeze. The two outer circular lines drawn around the form suggest the shape of a cameo.

Cameo
#99 round pointed Hunt drawing, "MB"

"Portrait of Adam and Eve" is a linear gesture drawing of the two sitting among the trees. This sketch was done with a Hunt "Globe" #513, extrafine, bowl-pointed, steel pen. This pen is probably one of the largest that I have in my collection. It is great for a fluid, fine line and holds slightly more ink because of its large size. The bowl-shaped tip (which when viewed from the side resembles the shape of a spoon bowl) glides easily across the paper's surface. If you intend to experiment (which you should) with pen and ink on different types of paper, I would recommend you start out with this type.

This drawing was done without a pencil sketch or planning.

Portrait of Adam and Eve
Ink, drawn on Pentalic Paper for Pens

The ink sketch "Idle Hour" was done with a Hunt "Imperial" #101 very flexible, extrafine, round-pointed, steel pen. I find this flexible nib good for drawing and sketching; it's an all-purpose point that will render fine detailed lines as well as broader lines.

As for the drawing, it was hurriedly drawn and completed during a conversation. I wanted the action of the character and detail in the most important areas, which are the hands and face areas. The other areas of the body are left as a simple linear outline.

Idle Hour
Higgins drawing ink, drawn on plate-finish, Morilla artist's bristol pad #188

33

Crow Quill Points

The "quill" pen points, such as the Crow Quill, Hawk Quill, and Flexible Quill, are smaller in size and have superfine points that can easily produce delicate hair lines for detailed areas. Because of the smaller size of these quill points, special pen holders are needed to accommodate them, but I strongly recommend you work with these pen points because of the variety of lines they can produce.

As you use a crow quill, remember that it has a very sharp point and tends to dig into the paper surface. Cold-press or medium-grade paper surface fibers may clog the point, so use a paper with a hard, smooth surface and avoid a paper with a loose fiber content.

The crow quill pen must be occasionally dipped in a reservoir of ink to replenish its ink supply. Be aware that the amount of ink on the pen will affect its performance. This is not to say that when the point runs dry it will no longer work, but only that the more ink on the point, the heavier the ink line, and the heavier the ink line, the longer it will take to dry.

A little care should be taken when drawing with a "fully loaded" pen point. Fast jerks or sudden stops in the hand stroke motion could cause the ink to fly, spill, or drip off the tip. While sketching with a crow quill, take the time to make sure the point is performing to its best ability. I always have a clean, damp rag handy to periodically and carefully wipe off the dried ink buildup on the pen point. Remember, the ink will flow easier off of a clean point.

Orange Merchant
Hay Market, Boston
Crow quill and brush, India ink, drawn on plate-finish, Morilla artist's bristol pad #188

These illustrations were all created in the same manner. First I lightly sketched them out on paper with a graphite pencil, then I used a crow quill to trace over the pencil line. As with "Memory of a Stray" on page 36, I elected to use the crow quill because of the range of linear effects achievable with this tool. Once that was complete, I gently removed the graphite line with a kneaded eraser, without scratching or reducing the dark tone of the India ink. Then I planned out the black areas, keeping in mind both depth and balance; I used a small round tip brush to fill the inked areas. This particular group of drawings may seem "flat" because there are no intermediate values; the only tones other than the dark ones are created by the linear areas. But even though the drawings appear flat, the black areas create visual depth. These dark areas were applied sparingly, because I didn't want them to overwhelm the drawn line.

Searching for Change ▶
Crow quill nib, India ink, drawn on Pentalic Paper for Pens

The Peanut Man ▼
Hay Market, Boston
Crow quill, India ink, drawn on 4 ply, plate-finish bristol board

Memory of a Stray
Crow quill nib, India ink, drawn on plate-finish bristol board

I chose a crow quill pen for this montage (this technique is described in Part Two, page 104) because I wanted a loose, flexible line.

You can see how flexible the crow quill is in drawing line lengths. The detailing in the cheek areas, the trees, the shading on the building and around the eyes show you how fine a line is possible. The whiskers illustrate the longer crow quill line, resulting from more ink and pressure on the nib.

The superfine point of the nib is especially suited to rendering the delicate crosshatched lines that add shading and form to the piece.

The Boy
*Magazine spot illustration.
Crow quill nib, waterproof India ink, drawn on Pentalic Paper for Pens*

The crow quill's normal line quality, which you can see in "Hay Market Butchers, Boston," right, is produced with a light to medium amount of pressure. This illustration is mainly composed of long lines and linear shading. In comparing this illustration to the "The Boy" spot illustration, below left, you can see the difference in the line. "The Boy" is mostly composed of fluid pen strokes, pushing the crow quill pen point to the maximum pressure. To create this fluid stroke you should exert pressure on the tip when the pen point first touches the paper, then pull the stroke downward, and ease up a bit on the slight upward swing. By holding the maximum amount of ink on the pen point, you can make about five or six of these strokes before dipping the pen into the ink reservoir. In the leaf area of "The Boy," a few telltale tracks of where the pen ran out of ink are still visible—they look like two small parallel lines. (These lines show how much the nib of the pen point was separated as a result of the large amount of pressure I applied.) If you study the drawing you can tell it was done by a right-handed person (which I am) because of the stroke direction and the pressure points on the stroke. This is obvious in the leaf strokes by the figure's head. The leaf area, believe it or not, took a long time to finish. Because so much ink was deposited on the paper, it took about twenty minutes for each five or six strokes to thoroughly dry. The ink softened the paper so that the pen point, as it closed (by the easing of the pres-

sure applied) picked up pieces of the softened paper in its jaws.

This "heavy" illustration style is best suited for spot drawings or small vignettes—in other words it's more effective in small doses!

Hay Market Butchers, Boston
Crow quill nib, waterproof India ink, drawn on Charrette bristol board #980

Lettering Nib

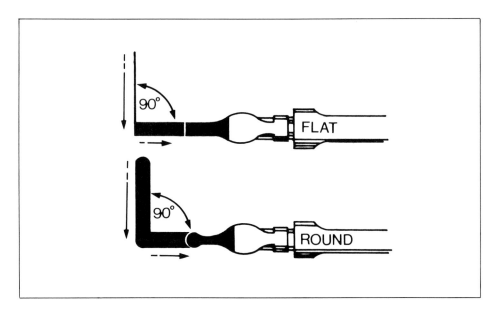

Here's a quick way to see the difference in the line between the round and the chisel edge of the lettering nib. Take a wide chisel lettering nib, dip it in ink, and from a point on the paper, draw a vertical line downward. Then without lifting the pen from the paper, make a 90-degree angle with the nib, creating a horizontal line. You'll notice the horizontal line is the same width as the nib, but the vertical line is much thinner. Now do the same with the round lettering nib—you'll find the vertical line is the same width as the horizontal. No matter what the angle, the line width will be consistent.

Lettering Nib

The lettering nib's main function in life, as the name implies, is to aid the artist in lettering and calligraphy. A lettering nib has a broader tip than a regular drawing nib and comes in a variety of shapes and sizes: flat or chisel-edge tips, oblique tips (angled for both left- and right-handed users), oval, and round tips.

The lettering nib certainly wasn't designed for sketching, but then neither were my fingers designed for typing. I enjoy sketching with a lettering nib because it gives me a nice fluid line, and the action in drawing is much faster than with a technical pen (see page 42). Plus it will produce a great variety of ink lines, depending on the width and shape of the nib used. A wider, heavier line is produced, which usually takes a little longer to dry because more ink is deposited on the paper. Some lettering nibs have metal clips that serve as an ink reservoir; this gives the pen greater ink capacity, a more uniform ink flow, and good ruling ability. You grip the pen holder in a natural way, just as you hold a pencil.

A variety of papers, parchments, and vellums can be used with these lettering nibs. For conventional lettering uses, a hard, smooth or light-toothed (hot-press) surface may suit your needs, but your best bet is to experiment with different paper types to see which one feels best to you.

The extended dot-dash line style illustration was rendered on a heavy vellum paper. The smooth, hard surface of this paper nicely accepts an ink line and allows me to use an electric eraser (which is the best tool for erasing ink). I drew the illustration without shading to accentuate the line detailing.

A "Platignum" lettering nib is unusual in that it does not have an ink clip and has a very fine, almost undetectable square edge. I continually dipped this nib and used it at all times with the maximum amount of ink on its tip, which accounts for the rounded ink line I received from it.

King Henry's Sixth Love
Platignum lettering nib, extrafine straight, waterproof India ink, drawn on Charrette Concept 900 paper

Reed Pen

The reed pen isn't meant for fine detail work as is the steel, manufactured pen point, because the reed can't be counted on for consistent line quality. No matter how thin the point may be carved, it will lay down a heavy ink line. This is because the amount of ink flow on the tip cannot be controlled. The ink may be absorbed into the wooden tip, or it may roll off the barrel and point all at once. The tip must be continually dipped into an ink reservoir, and for very heavy lines, this could mean the ink on the pen point may have to be replenished after every other pen stroke. "Why bother using a reed pen at all?" you ask. Well, I sometimes like the effect and the uncertainty a medium will give. Surprises are sometimes interest-

Reclining Nude
Drawn with reed pen and waterproof India ink on illustration board

This drawing was done with a slightly chiseled-edge reed pen and has a less "choppy" look to it than "Regina," opposite. Needless to say, the smaller the tip on a reed pen, the easier it is to control and vary the line widths. The different line widths in this drawing add interest to the drawn line. This drawing was first quickly sketched with a soft pencil for proportions and then inked over. A soft kneaded eraser was used to remove the pencil line after the ink had thoroughly dried. The illustration board I used gave me a good, smooth, yet hard and stiff drawing surface, which easily accepted the ink line.

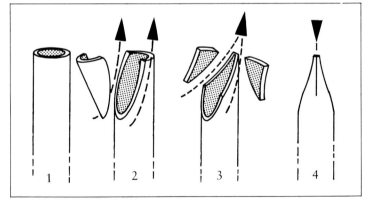

Reed pens are available commercially, or you can whittle your own from a thin stalk of bamboo into any shape, thickness, angle, or form. 1. Using a sharp penknife, first cut or trim the end so it is clean and straight. 2. Start about one-half inch from the end and push the knife away from you so it cuts through the reed in the middle of the reed. 3. About halfway up the first cut, again cut a new angle to the far edge. 4. Carefully slice vertically through the tip so the ink has a pathway to the tip and the paper surface; leave plenty of stalk for the handle.

ing, and an uninhibited approach can be very creative.

One of the reasons I became accustomed to using a reed pen was because the art school I attended was located in the South, where bamboo grows freely. It is a little different story living near Boston, where you can't walk into your back field to get a new supply of bamboo reed. Needless to say, to find thin bamboo reeds in the New England area took a bit of thought and a few telephone calls. My search finally ended at a garden supply store where I purchased a package of twenty-five, four foot bamboo tomato stakes. I was feeling so good about finding the elusive bamboo that I really wasn't listening to the sales clerk when he asked in a heavy Maine accent, "Grow'n tomatoes?" Now instead of going through the whole spiel about why I wanted the bamboo, I simply said, "Yep." Then my trouble started, because he asked, "What kind?" All I know about tomatoes is that you eat them, so I said, "The beefy ones." Bobbing his head up and down, he just said, "Oh." Even though he knew I didn't know what I was talking about, I still smiled all the way to my car because I had the bamboo under my arm.

The reed pen deposits large amounts of ink on the paper, and large amounts of ink means large amounts of moisture, so I recommend you use a bristol board, illustration board, or some other strong paper specifically designed to be used with ink. This paper thickness will reduce or eliminate the paper shrinkage that the moisture can cause which in turn could cause the paper to wrinkle or buckle.

For this almost gesture-like line drawing, I used two different sized reed pens to create the different line widths. The line widths were uncontrollable due to the large amount of ink on the tip of the reed.

On the wider border line series, I drew (on the average) only three lines before I had to replenish the ink. Care was taken in the ink application and placement of the border lines, so as not to drip the ink onto the paper. Much drying time was needed for each of these heavy ink strokes.

The narrower lines were then added. Little pressure was applied to the pen; it was placed gently on the paper and dragged lightly across the surface.

Because large amounts of ink were to be applied, a hard, thick bristol board was used to prevent wrinkling, warping, and paper shrinkage.

Regina
Drawn with a reed pen and waterproof India ink on Charrette bristol board #980

Technical Pen

The technical pen is primarily designed for tight, board work, which requires perfect rules or straight lines, and often uses a straightedge, T-square, or triangle.

The technical pen is a timesaving and very accurate tool since you don't have to constantly dip into a well of ink. The fine filament wire in the point allows a continuous flow of ink, which keeps surface friction to a minimum. The pen contains its own ink reservoir, making filling and cleaning easy.

The technical pen is considered a more controlled tool since it must be held vertical to the drawing paper in order to produce the best line quality.

Available in stainless steel, tungsten, or jewel points, the pens come in a variety of point sizes. Unlike other pen points, such as crow quill or lettering nibs, any given technical pen point produces a line weight that's basically consistent. Line widths range from .13mm to 2mm. (Some people refer to the .13mm as a 6 × 0, and the 2mm as a No. 7, so don't let this throw you.) Some technical pen brand names are FaberCastell, Rapidograph, Staedtler-Mars, Koh-I-Noor, Pentel, Pelikan, and K&E Leroy. Because these pens tend to be very expensive, regular cleaning is a must, but with proper care they should last a long time. (But don't apply too much pressure to a technical pen or it could snap off or severely bend the steel hypodermic tip.)

The best papers to use with a technical pen are the hard, smooth, hot-press types that render clean, crisp, accurate lines. The India inks specially formulated for technical pen use are free and easy flowing for even lines, dry quickly (the waterproof inks will not smear or smudge), and produce a dense, opaque black that renders excellent reproductions. I must confess, when I'm in a pinch, I'll use regular everyday waterproof India ink in my technical pens, and it always seems to work just as well.

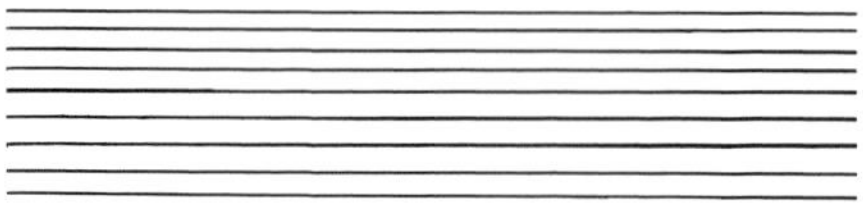

#0000 Technical Pen

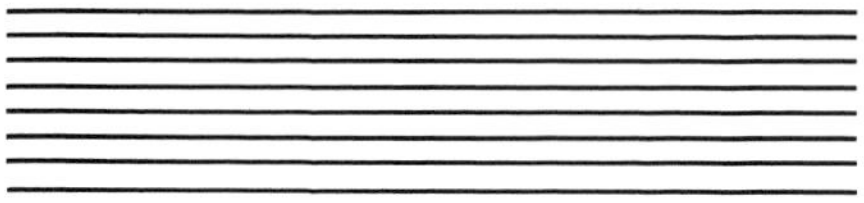

#00 Technical Pen

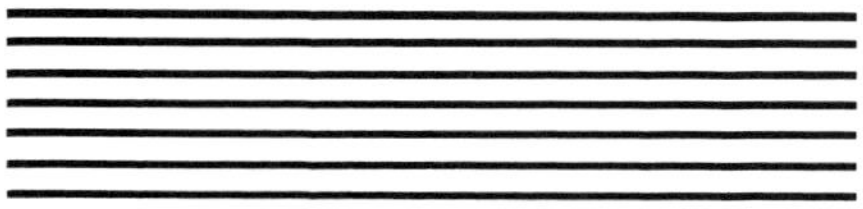

#2 Technical Pen

The technical pen, unlike other pen points, creates a line consistent in both density and width. You can buy technical pen points that can draw line widths ranging from .13mm to 2mm. The illustration above shows you some technical pen line variations.

Cleaning a Technical Pen

Remember: To perform to the best of their ability, technical pens must be *very* clean. The tendency is just to set the pen down after you've finished using it, but if you leave it for any length of time with an ink-filled cartridge, some of the ink may dry, and it may not produce a fluid line when you pick it up next time.

I've often found myself in this spot, because I hate the job of cleaning technical pens. I'll spend half an hour shaking and prodding my pen, literally pleading for it to work, rather than clean it. That's because technical pen points are a little tricky to clean. If you wash them by hand, you need to be careful not to harm or bend the fine, hairlike filament inside the point when taking it apart. Now I use an ultrasonic cleaner with a specially designed liquid soap, which will easily and quickly clean a fully assembled or disassembled technical pen point. Ultrasonic cleaners range in price from $30 to $100, so if you use a technical pen very often, consider investing in one. In any case, prevention is the best medicine; it's better to clean the pen *after* you use it, so you don't end up throwing it at the wall in frustration next time.

Any object that's shiny or has a high-gloss finish is going to have a reflective surface. The extreme variation between light and dark on shiny surfaces is referred to as a high contrast area. It's either black or white, with a possible line around, through, or beside to show the shape or form of the object. For example, take the right fender of the Packard: the black reflection of the headlight on the fender is bordered immediately by white. The center seam and also the curved form of the fender is defined by a simple line that flows downward into wavy horizontal lines; these horizontal lines could be used to indicate the fender's form, but in this case they're simply an indication of reflections from the surrounding landscape. The black area at the bottom of the fender represents reflections of the immediate foreground. Thus the fender goes from black at the top to white and then back again to black at its base, with only linear variation in between; no other intermediate tonal values appear between the whites and blacks.

Packard
#0 technical pen and waterproof India ink drawn on Charrette Concept 900 paper. Reproduced at 1.5 times original size.

This is one of the fun illustrations where anything goes and a variety of tools and art mediums was used. First, I used a #0 technical pen to complete the line drawing (other than the picture frame and what's in it). Using the same pen, a triangle, and T-square I added the vertical and horizontal crosshatch lines in the two figures.

Next, on another sheet of paper, I drew the picture frame with the same technical pen and the nude inside it with waterproof India ink and a #0 watercolor brush.

When you want to combine two pieces of art as I did here, the best way is to use a light table or box. This lets you position both pieces much more easily. For this illustration I placed the picture frame over the line drawing and carefully cut and trimmed the frame around the plants and the woman's head. I adhered the frame to the line drawing with spray adhesive.

For additional tone and textures, I mixed acrylic gel medium with the waterproof India ink and painted in the triangular shapes. This acrylic tone was also added in back of the two figures to separate and pop the figures out of the background.

Brunch with Delila
Drawn with a #0 (.35mm) technical pen, a #0 Grumbacher 3017 Camel Hair watercolor brush and waterproof India ink on Charrette Concept 900 paper. Triangular tones painted on with waterproof India Ink and Liquitex (tube) Acrylic Gel Medium. Mounted on 2 ply plate-finish bristol board

These could be referred to as "high contrast" illustrations because of their stark black-and-white areas. In the "Statue of Liberty" I took the graphic one step further and "stylized" it, accenting the outward form by drawing lines parallel to the darks. Although the subjects are greatly simplified, the graphic design of these illustrations makes them bold enough to stand on their own. (This is known as the hard edge graphic style and is covered in Part Three, page 142.)

Statue of Liberty *and* Woman with Hat
Drawn with waterproof India ink on plate-finish, Morilla artist's bristol board paper

Ballpoint Pen

A big advantage to ballpoint pens as drawing implements is that they're always available. And not only is the ink source built in, but all types of paper accept ballpoint ink. The ink flow is instantaneous, which gives you a fluid, free flowing line.

The ballpoint and technical pen are as different as night and day. The technical pen is held in an upright vertical fashion to produce a crisp, clean, accurate line. This line is applied with a slow precise motion. And since technical pens have been known to clog up from time to time, they need to be pampered. The ballpoint, on the other hand, is rugged, disposable, and inexpensive. They're also easy to find: if you're like me, you probably have a drawer somewhere filled with ballpoints you've found, bought, or borrowed from a sales person, then absentmindedly walked off with.

The ballpoint line can be drawn quickly, and the pen is held in a more comfortable position in the hand. The main disadvantage is that ballpoint pen ink takes longer to dry—sometimes up to two days. So in order to avoid smearing as you work across your drawing, lay a piece of clean paper over all the drawn areas. You can also use a corner of this protective overlay paper to wipe off any excess ink that builds up on the tip of a ballpoint pen. Otherwise, the ink may blob up on your drawing and give you an undesirable line. This happens frequently with the medium or broader tip ballpoints.

The fine-point PaperMate is one of my favorite types for sketching, but whether I use a medium or fine point depends on the size of the drawing I'm doing. Larger sketches call for a medium point, smaller ones for a fine point. Your best bet is to throw a few lines down on a sheet of scrap paper to really test the line thickness, because sometimes I can't tell the difference between a fine point and a medium even when I test them. I've often wanted to write and ask the manufacturers, "Fine and medium width—compared to *what* width?"

Shading with a pen and ink or ballpoint line can be accomplished with a close series of vertical lines, horizontal lines, or both, which is called *crosshatching*. The closer these lines are to each other, the darker the tone appears. (The alternative is to introduce a totally different media that can easily render different tonal gradations such as graphite, charcoal, different tones of felt-tips, or ink wash.)

The big advantage of ballpoint is that it will perform on virtually any paper you happen to have at hand, with the possible exception of a rough-surfaced watercolor paper. But in general, a paper with a slight tooth will work just as well as a plate-finish paper. The only noticeable difference is that the paper with the slight tooth may put a little drag on the pen.

I do sketches in ballpoint strictly for my own enjoyment, and the lines in the drawings reflect that. In the many years I've been drawing and illustrating, I've never used a ballpoint pen illustration for final art. I guess that's because I like to submit a more refined drawing—more polished, less coarse—as final art. But who knows, someday even that may change.

The main portion of this drawing—the man and the wooden bench he was sitting on—was done on the spot in about forty-five minutes. The pen I was using at the time was one of my favorite types for sketching—a black Paper-Mate ballpoint, fine nib. The big advantage of having a ballpoint handy is that it will perform on virtually any type of paper you happen to have at hand—with the possible exception of a rough-surfaced paper such as a watercolor paper.

A plate-finish paper's surface works just as well as a paper with a slight tooth. The only noticeable difference between the two is that the paper with the slight tooth may put a little drag on the pen.

By the Newport Beach
PaperMate ball, fine nib, black,
drawn on plate-finish, Morilla
artist's bristol pad #188

The "Studies of Three Birds" are just that, three working studies that were quickly drawn with the ballpoint. Some of the preliminary "construction" lines are still seen because the ballpoint I used had nonerasable ink. The speed with which these were done captures the life, character, and basic shapes of the birds. In the owl, a circular line was first drawn, which immediately established the face and head area, then its body was added (and extended from the circular drawn line) with a series of quick, oval feathers. The chickadee, bottom, was drawn as it darted back and forth from a bowl of seed at my window, and the sketch lines are more prominent because of its constant movement. The flycatcher, top, was a good model, sitting quite still on its nest, which only appears as a mere indication. The detail and linear tone were kept mainly in its head and body to draw and hold the viewer's attention.

Studies of Three Birds
Bic ball, fine nib, black, drawn on Strathmore series 300 paper

Since the ballpoint medium will produce only line, without tone gradations, any shading must be done with a series of close parallel and crosshatching lines or by introducing another totally different medium such as graphite, charcoal, felt-tip, or ink wash. This sketch shows how you can use quick and loose lines to simplify areas. Bothersome detail areas were eliminated because I mainly wanted to capture the shape and overall form created by the landscape.

Maine Landscape
PaperMate ball, medium nib, black, drawn on Attica sketch paper

Crosshatching is the criss-crossing of lines to add value and build tone. The three basic lines—horizontal, vertical and diagonal—are shown in the left column. You can see the tone that results from combining these lines in the right column.

Felt-Tip Pen and Marker

Felt-tip pens and marker nibs have greatly improved and become increasingly harder since their invention with the use of more durable materials such as felt, nylon, vylon, plastic, and foam. The nibs stay sharp and firm, and deliver an even flow for superb line quality.

Nibs vary in thickness and shape; the most common are the fine-line writing and heavier, chisel- or wedge-shaped markers well suited for lettering and drawing. The uses of these markers vary widely from sketching to making a fast yard sale sign to comprehensive, color layouts for an ad or brochure. AD Markers even have interchangeable nibs, some of which (wedge and brush) you can chisel and notch with a very sharp razor blade to create different lines. Markers with double ends offer the convenience of broad and fine nibs in one pen. Brush markers have soft

foam nibs usable as both brushes and markers.

Those pens with non-water-soluble inks are permanent and dry instantly. But alcohol-based inks are considered toxic and should be used in a well-ventilated room only. Some non-water-soluble felt-tip types are AD markers (which are available in 200 permanent colors), Eberhard Faber Design Art Marker, Berol Prismacolor Art Markers (double-ended markers), and Pantone Color Markers (203 colors).

Water-soluble markers are nontoxic and odorless. Some of the water-soluble markers, however, aren't permanent and the ink tends to smudge if you rub over it. To prevent such a disaster, most likely if you're working in the warm sunshine and your hand or wrist becomes moist, use the paper overlay method discussed on page 47. Also, impermanent inks seem to

dry rather slowly. My experience with STABILayout 38 markers (water-based) is that they may take up to an hour to dry on the paper.

Markers come in a kaleidoscope of colors that include brights, pastels, and fluorescents. Some water-based types are STABILayout and Stabilo Pen markers, Marvy markers, Pentel Fine-Point Color Pens, and Eberhard-Faber Design Chisel Points, to name just a few. The FaberCastell Textliner for highlighting text is one of many brands of felt-tips that come in fluorescent colors. Another water-soluble marker type is the brush marker, Marsgraphic 3000 Brush Markers, which has a soft, flexible, foam tip. This marker can be used both as a marker or a brush and works well for drawing fine lines or wide, bold strokes and is ideal for blending and shading.

I drew over my pencil sketch with a water-soluble Pilot Razor Point for a black, thin line. Using a waterproof Stanford Sharpie I darkened in the black and shadow areas in the drawing. The Sharpie is the best tool for this task because of its rounded tip. It produces a nice, permanent, broad line and is much easier to use in the tighter, smaller areas of the drawing. If you used the broad, "squared off" or "chiseled edge" markers they would prove harder to handle and more cumbersome.

Conversation with John, the Long Rider
Sketched with a "B" graphite pencil, then drawn with a Pilot

Razor Point and shaded with a Stanford Sharpie on Pentalic Paper for Pens

This line drawing was completed with a water-soluble marker and no water wash was intended to be used with it. Shading was used sparingly, and contour, linear shading (some crosshatching) was used. It's nice to combine a fast, flowing line (and not have to continually return to the ink bottle to replenish the ink supply) with drawing speed, on a nice, smooth, plate-finish paper.

Amish Barn
Black, Pilot Razor Point drawn on Pentalic Paper for Pens

The illustration was first very lightly sketched out with a soft graphite pencil then drawn over with a water-soluble Pilot Razor Point felt-tip pen.

After the drawing was complete, most of the darkest tone areas were added first with an Eberhard-Faber Design Chisel Point #492, which is a water-based lettering marker with a plastic, chisel-shape point. I then switched to alcohol-based felt tips for the remaining tones. If I continued to use water-soluble markers there was a chance they would dissolve the lines in the drawing. For the background tones I used three different AD markers by Chartpak. A #1 Cool Grey #P181, a #2 Cool Grey #P182 and a #3 Cool Grey #P183. Both the wide and narrow parts of the markers were used.

When all of the line and tones in the drawing had been completed using the felt tips, I still needed an interesting design or repeated pattern in the background to balance the weight of the front tires. In my mind's eye, I kept seeing a repeated pattern and the best way to create that feeling was with a stencil. I used the aerosol technique described on page 96 to create the background.

The Easy Winner
Drawn with a Pilot Razor Point and shaded with #1 and #3 cool gray AD Markers. Trees sprayed with black enamel spray paint

I first lightly sketched this house with a soft leaded pencil. After the basic proportions and areas were in, I switched to a new, water-soluble black Razor Point felt-tip pen to draw the final lines and linear detailing. This freehand line was purposely left alone so the linear character, details, and personality of the house would not be diminished by secondary shading and tone. The drawing of the house proceeded nicely, and I stopped working on it when I reached the lower right hand corner of the building and then took off. In its planning stages I knew I wanted an object in the foreground of the picture to visually help take the viewer back into the background areas but not interfere or greatly cover the line in the background.

Back in the studio, I continued with the line drawing, adding a little action to it by adding the linear figure of an older man, walking, and vignetted the brick street to keep him from floating. Something was wrong; I needed definition in the line between the house and man because both blended together. I then grabbed the handiest thing I could find for tone, which was a Mars Graphic 3000 felt-tip (whose shape resembles a pointed brush) and applied a medium tone in the suit of the man, and voilà! It was just what I was looking for. After a day of letting the drawing dry, I softly removed the pencil line with the kneaded eraser.

After the Market
Black, Pilot Razor Point and #85 Mars Graphic 3000 felt-tip, drawn on Pentalic Paper for Pens

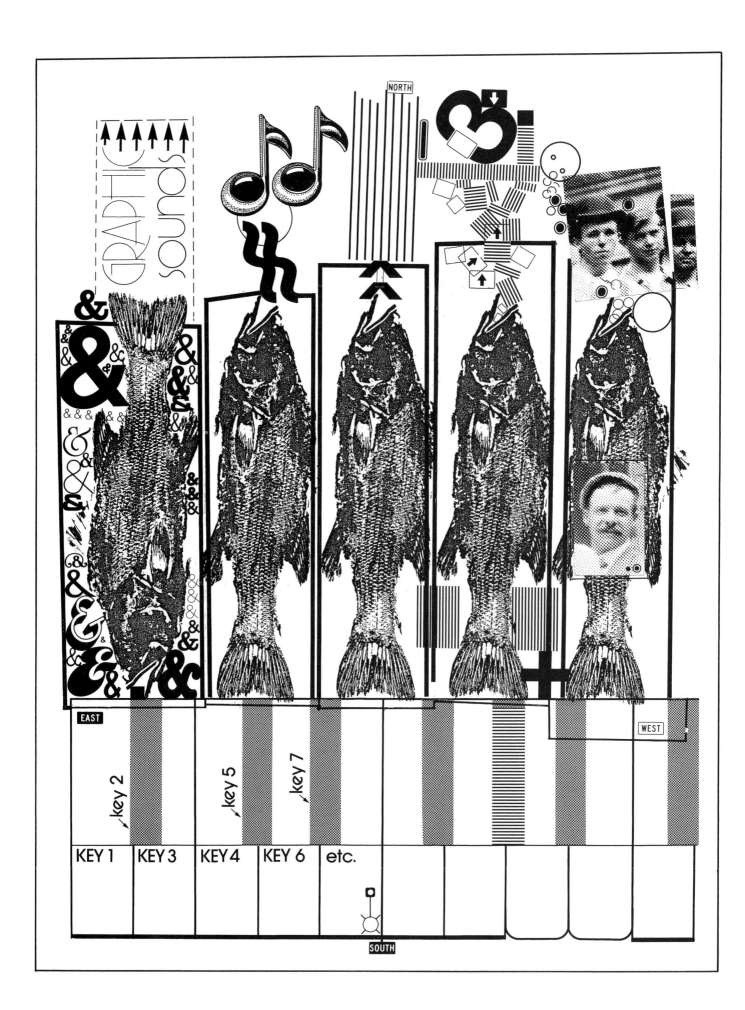

PART TWO

TECHNIQUES

P art Two covers the manner in which the art mediums or medium combinations are applied. Technique may determine or dictate the end result, which is called the art style. You can learn a lot from other artists, and now is a good time to look around and see how other artists have worked. Examine their drawings, break them down, examine their thinking processes, styles, techniques, tonal qualities, subject matter, and how they convey the feeling or mood in their visuals.

Again, I stress that experimentation is the basis for creativity. Don't be afraid to break the rules; try anything and everything once, maybe just to see what happens and why it happens, and then analyze why it turned out the way it did. I'm always playing a "what if" game with my art. What if I add a wash over the pencil line, what if I scumble a charcoal line near the center of interest, will I blow it? I won't know until I try. I may have a good idea whether it will work, but even if I ruin it, there are probably several things I can do to try to save it from the big garbage can in the sky. I experiment constantly with my art work. Of course, I realized many years ago that every piece of art that I produce may not turn out to be a masterpiece or may not even be successful, and I must confess I am not afraid to "blow an illustration out of the water," for the sake of experimentation. You can bet your last dollar, next time I'll be a little smarter because of the experiment, knowing what to do or what not to do or how to do it better. Experiment with your art work and don't be afraid to try different things at least once. After all, you may find you like the way it turned out, and at the same time, you may have discovered a whole new avenue of techniques and styles for your art.

Fish Organ
Collage, pasted on 2 ply,
plate-finish bristol board

Scumbling with a Pencil

For this quick five-minute sketch I used the side of the pencil lead instead of its point. Shading was quickly added and indicated with the scumbled line.

Nude Study
Graphite, Ebony pencil drawn and scumbled on gray bond paper

To *scumble* in painting involves laying a light, semitransparent color on a surface already painted with another color to unify or soften the area and create textural quality. But you can also produce a scumbled line with graphite by using the side of the lead rather than the point; charcoal, Conté, and pastel will work as well. In drawing, scumbling gives a rougher, more textural look. I use this technique frequently for quick sketches or visual notes, and sometimes to shade areas within a line drawing, as I did in "Bill's Investment," opposite.

When you draw in the conventional manner with the pencil's point, the side of your hand—and possibly your wrist and arm—are actually touching the paper's surface. But because scumbling is done with the side of the pencil rather than the point, you don't rest your wrist on the paper. To scumble, position your paper or drawing surface one to two feet in front of you on an easel or propped-up drawing board; the paper should be vertical or at a 45-degree angle. This slight reach will give your wrist the freedom of movement you need to make a scumbled line.

The easiest way to scumble is to hold the pencil between your thumb and forefinger with the pencil body inside your hand, near or touching your palm. Experiment with holding your pencil in different ways to produce different scumbling effects. Also try applying different amounts of pressure for varying tones, but be aware that too much pressure may snap off the point.

A light- to medium-tooth paper produces the best results, because this tooth provides a better surface for the medium to adhere to. The scumbled line can pick up the character of the paper, which adds even more interest to the line. A slick or very rough paper surface may make the pencil slide or skip, reduce adhesion of the medium, and create an undesirable "missed" effect. Experiment with different papers to see the difference in the scumbled line.

The base line drawing in this illustration was done in the conventional way, with the pencil's point, which accounts for the slight difference in the look of the line. All the shaded areas were then scumbled, particularly in Bill's face where I used very light pencil pressure to slowly and carefully build up the dark value.

Bill's Investment
"BBB" Wolff's carbon pencil, drawn and scumbled on Strathmore series 300 paper

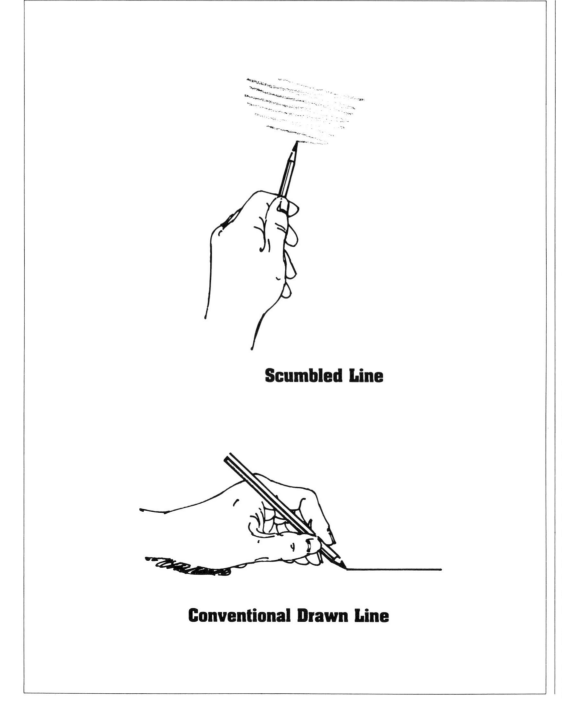

Scumbled Line

Conventional Drawn Line

The illustration, left, shows how the pencil is comfortably held to produce a scumbled line with a back and forth, fluid motion. Notice that the scumbled line is produced with the side of the pencil lead rather than its point.

Scumbling is easily done with the paper or drawing surface placed in a vertical manner, such as on an easel. Compare this to the conventional (writing) way of holding the pencil. The line is produced with the pencil's point.

In this preliminary sketch, right, the quickly scumbled graphite line is used primarily to indicate values, and particularly the shadow areas of the girl's forehead. The lines in the girl's shoulder and hair are continuous; you can see how I scumbled here with rapid, continuous pencil strokes. Although the scumbling in this piece isn't labored over, it does add a little motion to what would otherwise be a static subject.

Young Girl with Roses
Graphite, "B" lead, drawn and scumbled on Hammermill bond pad 940

Gesso-Surface Technique

Gesso is a water-soluble, liquid-ground coating used primarily to prepare a canvas surface for oil painting. Gesso is opaque, dries in minutes, adheres to most surfaces, dries with a brilliant whiteness, and does not yellow with age. This coating also provides an excellent tooth for charcoal, graphite, or Conté line art.

Use the gesso as it comes right from the jar or container; it's mixed and ready to go. Choose a sturdy paper or board that won't buckle or warp when the gesso has dried on it. Because of the opaque whiteness of the gesso, you can use all types of cardboard (the cardboard doesn't necessarily have to be white). I save and use the cardboard ends of my paper pads or an illustration or drawing board. If I'm going to prepare a sample piece for my portfolio, I'll use a piece of 2 ply bristol board. Just be sure to tape down the four corners of

This drawing was first lightly sketched on the gesso-prepared paper; then the broader line finished the illustration.

Generally when you work on a gesso-prepared surface, you'll use light sketch lines to first draw and map out your drawing; these lines will disappear as they blend in with any heavier or broader lines you add later. I often combine both the pencil line and scumbling in an illustration on a gessoed surface, and usually I'll try to employ one or more large, dark areas in a drawing. These dark areas are planned to take full advantage of and show the texture and characteristics of the gesso-surface lines, which were made by the coarse brushstrokes.

On the Lunar Surface
"B" Wolff's charcoal pencil, drawn on a gesso-prepared surface

In this drawing, "Against the Current," the uses of the pencil are more easily seen. The detail areas in the head, chest, and the figure's right hand are more finished and refined than the rest of the drawing, since these are the key areas. The farther down you travel visually, the looser and sketchier the drawn line becomes, which emphasizes both these areas of primary interest and the movement I wanted in the piece. The figure's suit is only indicated and is very simplified. Unlike most of the drawing, I rendered the fins with just one line, adding dark scumbling within their outline to add to the sense of water movement or cur-

rent. The lightly scumbled lines that extend from the figure's right hand over his right leg and stop at the fins, were also added for this reason.

Against the Current
"B" Wolff's carbon pencil, drawn on a gesso-prepared surface

the bristol board to something flat (like a drawing board) before you brush on the gesso; this will help the bristol board dry flat.

To prepare your surface for line art, use a two-inch or three-inch, inexpensive nylon bristle brush because the heavy nylon bristles will add to the surface sculpture of the gesso coating. One *heavy* coat of gesso will do. Brush the gesso in long strokes and vary the angles of your strokes. Be careful not to end a stroke in the middle of the drawing area or it may create an undesirable buildup that will interrupt the free-flowing line to be drawn. After you've covered the paper with gesso, give it a good two to three hours to thoroughly dry. All of the moisture should be out of the cardboard, which may take even more drying time on humid days. If you try drawing on it while it's wet, you'll undoubtedly mess it up. And be sure to thoroughly wash out your nylon brush immediately—once the gesso dries, it becomes rock hard.

After your gesso is completely dry, you're ready to draw. Notice how the drawn line rides across the top ridges of the gesso coating and how the line picks up the grain of the gesso brushstroke.

In checking over your drawing, you may want to clarify or highlight certain areas. Highlighting can easily be done by lightly scratching the drawn-on gesso surface with a sharp knife or razor blade. Scratch in the direction of the gesso brushstroke, try not to scratch against the grain or you may chip off a chunk of gesso.

When you've finished your drawing, give the surface a light coat of fixative.

Dry Wash

This is by far one of my favorite techniques. Dry wash is versatile—you can use it not only to create subtle tone gradations but also to add movement to a drawing. And dry wash is adaptable; done in graphite, charcoal, chalk, pastels, or Conté, dry wash can be combined with other mediums to produce a variety of effects.

Each of the two basic ways of rendering a dry wash has its own distinctive look: the first plays up tone gradations, the second creates movement. But the preliminary procedure for both methods is the same. First you sketch your baseline drawing and lightly spray it with a workable fixative to protect it. (A permanent fixative will *not* work!) Then, on a separate piece of paper, scumble a large area to produce a graphite deposit and rub a rolled up facial tissue in the graphite. The darkness of the tone depends on the amount of graphite on the tissue; a little graphite will produce a light tone, while more graphite makes a darker tone. This is where the methods part company.

With the first method, to create tone gradations, you apply the graphite tissue to your drawing and *rub* in the areas you want toned. You don't have to worry about staying in the lines, because the next step is to take a kneaded eraser and clean up the areas you don't want toned. After you've done that, spray the drawing again lightly with workable fixative. The trick with this method is not to try and achieve darker tones all at once. Repeat the step of rubbing with the graphite tissue until you've built your tone to the desired darkness. Then you can erase the overflow areas, and spray again.

Each time the dry wash is applied,

the excess should be cleaned up with the kneaded eraser and then a *light* coat of workable fixative should be applied. This light coat of fixative will add permanence to each separate application of dry wash.

The second dry wash method creates a look of movement as well as some tone gradations, as seen in the "Basketball spot illustration," page 66. This method differs from the first in that you make only one stroke with the medium-prepared tissue instead of rubbing. The longer the stroke, the more gradation in tone. Move the tissue in the direction you want your subject to be traveling from and never rework or go back over the tone that you've made with a single swipe. However, if it looks bad, you can erase it and try again. Highlights and the other areas you don't want toned in can also be cleaned up with a kneaded eraser. Finish with a light coat of workable fixative.

Once you've mastered the basic dry-wash technique you may want to experiment with various other mediums. Try combining a graphite or charcoal dry wash with line drawings in ink, graphite, or charcoal. You can also cut a paper stencil for more controlled dry-wash tone areas or repeated design. The sole purpose of the paper stencil is to keep certain areas of the artwork clean.

The door, the doorway, the boy, and the brick walkway were drawn first; then I applied a light coat of workable fixative to protect the line art from smudging. Next, in order to keep the drawing relatively clean and free of hundreds of guide lines for the background brick, I devised an easy and clean method of rendering the brick on both sides of the door. On a separate sheet of paper, I drew a series of five rows of brick, then taped that sheet to a light table. By keeping the brick drawing taped down and stationary, I could position and reposition the drawing over it to cleanly trace the rows of brick. While tracing, I staggered some of the brick lengths and shapes to add a little interest and variety to the wall.

When the background brick was finished, I sprayed on another light coat of workable fixative for protection. Next I cut a paper stencil for the decorative fence and applied the dry wash. After I'd cleaned up the fence outline with a kneaded eraser, another light coat of workable fixative was applied. Now the illustration was really starting to take shape.

The last steps were to add the tones on the planned areas in the win-

dow, on the jacket, and walkway. With the same tissue I'd used for the fence, I freely applied the dry wash.

I used the charcoal dry wash technique primarily for balance and to lead the viewer's eye around. The dark tone areas—in the window at the top of the door, the jacket, the brick walkway, and the fence at the right—are strategically placed to form a triangular shape within the picture. The viewer's eye will fall on one of these three toned areas first, then travel to the second and third to see the entire drawing. The order in which these areas are viewed doesn't matter, just that these areas will be prominently seen.

Then I used the kneaded eraser to clean up the boy's shirt collar, pants, face, hands and hoe, and to remove all of the excess tone around the window. A final, light coat of workable fixative was applied.

Study of Fleroy
(for Yankee Magazine)
"BBB" Wolff's carbon pencil, drawn on Strathmore 300 series paper

This illustration combines carbon line with carbon dry wash in a fairly typical way. The big difference is in how the drawing's background was created.

After the line drawing was finished and fixed, I prepared my carbon deposit as described in the text. I took a large sheet of scrap paper and lightly taped it across the line drawing at elbow height of the figure to suggest a background horizon line, then rubbed my carboned tissue liberally around the shape of the figure on the line drawing. I spent a few minutes erasing the carbon I'd accidentally rubbed in the areas of the shirt and chair and gave the drawing a light coat of workable fixative. These steps were repeated until I was satisfied with the tonal darkness of the face shadow and background.

Next I wanted to define the shape of the head and separate it from the dark background. In theory, if I could use a paper stencil to make certain areas and designed shapes darker, I also could to the reverse and make areas lighter. So I reached for my pad of white bond paper, drew the outline shapes of people in a crowd, and cut out the stencil. The key was to use the positive or center part of the stencil and make the surrounding areas lighter from the darker, protected areas the stencil covered. After some patching of the stencil to ensure that it completely covered the man's head, I prepared a large amount of white pastel. I transferred the pastel medium deposit onto the tissue and was now ready to apply the white pastel medium to the background area.

Holding the paper stencil in place on the drawing with one hand, I worked all of the application strokes of the tissue from the center of the paper stencil outward, across the edge of the stencil and onto the black background. Sometimes it's difficult to keep a hand-held paper stencil flat. If the tissue strokes are applied from the background onto the paper stencil the tissue may accidentally pick up an end of the stencil, and the white pastel may get under the paper stencil. This would lead to a lot of unnecessary cleanup.

After I completed the white pastel dry wash, the stencil was removed and the sharp edges the stencil had created on the right side of the head were lightly feathered with the white pastel tissue. I sprayed on a light coat of workable fixative.

Then I removed the large sheet of paper I'd taped down to create the horizon line and lightly feathered the right side of this line with my carbon tissue. While I had the tissue in my hand, I added light tone areas to the shirt, pants, and just a hint of tone under the chair to prevent the figure from floating.

Finally, to visually tie the foreground figure in with the background, I cut a small paper-stencil circle and stenciled four separate thought bubbles from the figure's hat into the dark background. Then the entire illustration was given a light coat of workable fixative.

Woodstock Revisited
"BBB" Wolff's carbon pencil used for both line and dry wash, drawn on Hammermill bond paper

Basketball spot illustration
*Berol charcoal pencil, medium,
used for both line and dry wash,
drawn on Strathmore series 300
paper*

For the basketball illustration, left, I first put down the line art in charcoal and applied two separate coats of workable fixative to prevent smudging. I then decided to use the second dry-wash method on this illustration because I wanted a sense of movement. I began by preparing a large charcoal deposit on a piece of scrap paper, and dragged a wadded tissue across it to easily pick up the deposit onto the tissue with just the single swipe, instead of rubbing the tissue back and forth in the deposit. (This one-swipe action keeps the charcoal on the tissue's surface and it is deposited onto your drawing more easily.) I applied the dry wash to the areas where I wanted the tone to appear darkest and then pulled the tissue away from the object so the tone gradated and gave motion to the image.

(For example, if you were to draw a ball and wanted to show its motion traveling left to right, you'd place a prepared dry-wash tissue next to the left side of the ball and make a single swipe with the tissue to the left.)

I prepared the tissue separately each time a motion swipe was needed. After all of these motion tones were on the drawing, I checked them for tonality, erasing the excess tone that overlapped the line. Two separate light coats of workable fixative were sprayed on.

This illustration combines carbon dry wash with India ink line. I used a #1 technical pen (which produced a very smooth, fluid line) to render continuous lines and give shading and form to the garment, grass, and trees. After I'd completed the ink lines, I cut the center out of a large sheet of white bond paper, leaving about 6" of extra paper all around, and rounded the top corners. The stencil was positioned on top of the line drawing. After each dry-wash application, I lifted the stencil and checked tonality. I also created highlights by using a clean kneaded eraser to remove carbon from the areas where I didn't want tone and for general cleanup. A light coating of workable fixative was applied last.

Strictly for the Birds
Waterproof India ink and #1 technical pen line, used with a "BBB" Wolff's carbon pencil dry wash, drawn on Morilla artist's bristol pad #188

Stippling

Stippling closely resembles a halftone in that it's solely composed of tiny dots. Halftones are used to print photos in newspapers. Examine one under a magnifying glass, and you'll see the pattern of dots. Darker values result when the dots are close together; lighter values are created when the dots are farther apart. Stippling with a pen works the same way, and although it's a long and tedious process, it's not that difficult.

Stipple can be done in a variety of art mediums—felt-tips, charcoal, graphite, and paint to name just a few. Charcoal and graphite may be the hardest to use for stippling because the medium is harder to control and apply. Also, illustrations made with these mediums will not reproduce as well because they aren't as dark or strong as the ink or felt-tip dots. The Neo-impressionist artist, Georges Seurat, became famous for painting his canvases with a series of tiny color dots. The mind perceives these dots as a blend of colors. (It's well-documented that he died from exhaustion and overwork.)

In the long run, stippling is a worthwhile technique to master because it's compatible with just about every other style you can think of— line art or wash in India ink, graphite, charcoal, and Conté. The stipple technique is also a style in itself, and as you can see from the illustrations on these pages, it can be used successfully to picture everything from food to portraits—even landscapes.

To stipple with a technical pen, first pencil in your drawing on a sheet of white bond or heavy vellum. Tape this sketch to a light table, then place and tape or secure your drawing paper on top. Following your un-

The concept of this montage was to produce a portfolio piece and a sample of how easily ink line and stippled tones can be combined. The added stipple in this sample does double duty: it adds not only shading and tone to certain areas, but also interest to the line drawing.

At the Races
Waterproof India ink used with a #1 technical pen for line and stipple on Pentalic Paper for Pens

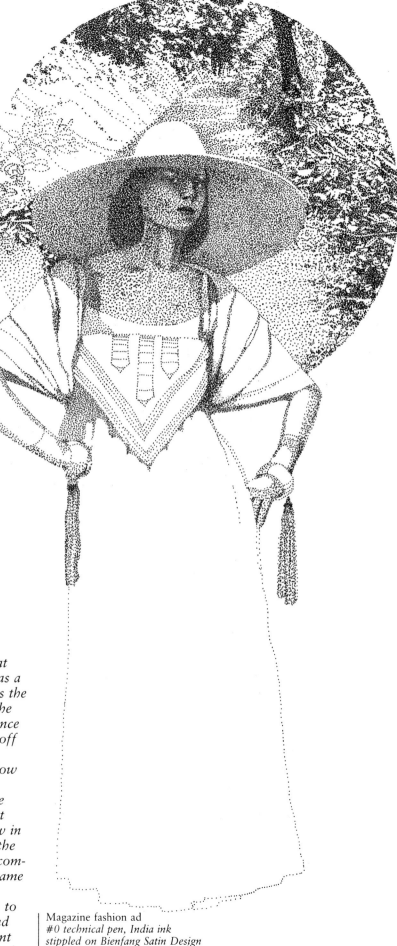

This illustration was used as a half-page magazine ad for a "clothes revival" shop. After I'd penciled the figure on a sheet of white paper, I taped this drawing onto a light table; a sheet of Bienfang, Satin Design 150 was then secured over it. (Bienfang Satin Design paper has a smooth tooth surface similar to Pentalic Paper for Pens.) Using a #0 technical pen and waterproof India ink, I began stippling the entire figure area. The key at this point was not to go very dark in any of the stippled areas. To avoid overworking the drawing, I took frequent breaks to check its progress.

After the entire figure was stippled, I went back over the drawing and fine-tuned some areas by slowly darkening and balancing them with one another.

The background's tonal darkness was dictated by the darkness of the hat shadow area. A delicate balance had to be found between these areas, because if the background was too dark it would overpower the hat shadow.

As I was lightly stippling in the background landscape, I found I could go slightly darker on top of the hat and create a white border around the brim of the hat to visually separate both tone areas. I could leave the background at the top left of the hat as a negative space (perhaps the bank of a hill, which the sun is hitting) and bounce the hat shadow nicely off of that.

I left the lower shadow and tonal shape in the background around the bottom parts of the hat lighter than the shadow in the hat, to accentuate the hat's shadow without competing with it. At the same time, I could create a three-dimensional look to the figure's garment and visually pop the garment out from the background.

Magazine fashion ad
#0 technical pen, India ink
stippled on Bienfang Satin Design
150

derlying sketch, lightly stipple the entire drawing; you can come back later and rework to balance the tone areas. It's disastrous if a stippled area gets too dark because it may dictate all the surrounding tones, making the whole picture too dark—not to mention all that extra stippling!

Take short, frequent breaks to check your progress and make sure you aren't overworking an area. Turn off the light in the light table, untape the top edge of the drawing paper and, with the other three sides still taped in place, slip a sheet of white paper between the penciled sketch and the stippled drawing. This helps whiten the stippled sheet of paper, blocking out and removing any darker shadows created by the underlying graphite line. To proceed with stippling, simply remove the middle sheet, retape the top of the paper, turn the light back on, and proceed.

Because stippling is such tight and tedious work, done at such close range, after a while you may begin to suffer eye strain. Rest your eyes as often as you need to. The best way to relax your eyes is to focus on the farthest thing from you, perhaps a tree out the window or a picture on the opposite wall. Stare at this for a while, and you'll actually feel the muscles in your eyes relax.

One note here about the uses of the stipple technique: Remember this technique takes a lot of everything—time, patience, persistence, and eye strength. My stipple illustrations are usually small, spot illustration size (under 6″ × 6″), because I don't want to drive myself crazy by spending a month and a half on one drawing—besides, what client could afford it?

Every phase of this illustration was carefully planned; it combines the stipple technique with ink lines. Stipple line is used to frame secondary interest points at the top and bottom. The primary focal point, the ice cream cone, is entirely stippled. After I'd completed the ice cream it looked too solid. I reworked these areas with Pro White and a no. 1 red sable brush to add a little more texture and dimen- *sion. Pro White is very opaque and corrects the India ink line with ease. I rendered the type last to complete the illustration.*

Chocolate Fix
#1 technical pen with waterproof India ink stippled on Pentalic Paper for Pens

In this drawing for a magazine ad you can see how I used spattering (ink or other medium placed on a toothbrush and spattered onto the paper) to create a stipple-like effect. Spattering is a quicker way to achieve this effect. This stipple effect was used primarily to "frame in" and accentuate (pop out) the soft, graphite line subject.

One of the main reasons stippling is so compatible with other styles and techniques is that tone darknesses can be greatly varied and won't overwhelm the other mediums it's used with.

If you look closely and analyze other illustrations in this book, you'll see how the stipple technique complements other mediums in its subtle way.

Magazine art for restaurant ad
India ink stippled and combined with 2B graphite line, drawn on Morilla artist's bristol pad #188

Drawing with a Brush and Ink

Drawing with a brush has its advantages. The brush bristles act as an ink reservoir, which means you can work the brush wet or dry. The brushstroke or line thickness depends on the thickness of the brush, the amount of medium the brush is holding, and the angle or pressure of your brushstroke.

Normally when I sketch with a brush, I expect a clean, fluid line. I keep the brush full of ink; when it runs low, I simply dip the brush in the ink again. This is a constant process with wet-brush technique. Dry-brush occurs when the brush is pushed to the limit and beyond—when very little ink is left in the brush.

The dry-brush technique creates a "skipped" or "missed" effect that adds texture and tonal variety to your drawings. Dry-brush can be done successfully on the supersmooth, plate-finished papers, as well as on most medium-tooth papers, but too much texture will interfere with the dry brushstroke. Use very thick ink, as thick as possible. (Leave a bottle of ink open to the air for a day or two and it'll thicken up.)

It's not difficult to control the dry brush in drawing as long as the dryness of the brush is kept fairly consistent. Remember, this isn't a wet wash; the brush must be dry enough to achieve the tones you're after. You'll need plenty of scrap paper to work the excess ink out of your brush before applying it to a drawing.

One of the advantages of dry-brush is that it can be lightly reworked if, at first, the brush areas are kept relatively soft and dry. The same line can be brushed over and over again, to achieve the desired darkness. The only problem with this technique is the unconscious tendency to overwork a sketch by going back over the dry-brush lines with a newly dipped brush, which adds a more fluid line and destroys the spontaneous dry-brush areas. You can avoid this disaster by always using scrap paper to test the dampness of your brush.

Keep your dry-brush sketches looking crisp by leaving a variety of dry-brush strokes and areas in them. This variety may be achieved by varying the thicknesses, lengths, directions or contours, and tone darknesses of the brushstrokes. Also, remember to make your brushstrokes in the right direction: they should follow the con-

This cartoon illustration was done with a round brush and ink (see pages 150-151 for cartoons rendered in technical pen). Notice that definition of forms, shading, and humorous emphasis are all accomplished with the varying width and length of the brushstrokes.

Magazine cartoon illustration
India ink used with a no. 2 round liner brush, drawn on Charrette Concept 900

In this quick sketch you can easily spot the starting points where the brush was full of India ink as well as the areas where the brush ran dry. I dipped the brush twice for this drawing. After first dipping the brush, I indicated the right side of the figure's torso with a quick line. Next I added the lower left torso line, swung up to the top right shoulder, and drew my basic oval for the head. While the brush still had a little life left in it, I quickly sketched the face, added some of the hair, and indicated some of the shadow lines around the lower throat. At this point the brush was almost dry; it ran completely dry in the model's hair area. After dipping the brush for the second time, I immediately indicated the left arm and armpit then swung up to the top of the model's hair, filling in the darker areas around the face. The sketch was finished in about six minutes, and while the model dozed off for twenty minutes or so, I managed to rip off five quick sketches from my pad.

Sleeping Model
Waterproof, India ink dry brush, drawn on Hammermill bond paper

tour or shape of what is being drawn. Random strokes look out of place and unnecessary.

Wet and dry brushstrokes can be easily combined in a drawing or painting. This is readily seen in paintings ranging from watercolors and oil paintings to dye or ink brush drawings. Just about every type of art medium that uses a brush for its application will have a combination of wet and dry brushstrokes. This occurs naturally because it is a characteristic of the brush to use up the limited amount of art medium it can hold at one time and go dry.

Red sable brushes produce good results with dry-brush, but you may like the dry-brush effect that stiffer brushes produce. You may choose the camel-hair or bristle brushes over the red sable; the price may also have a bearing on your choice, because the prices on the red sable brushes are outrageous.

Brush and Palette

Most brushes have certain specific functions to perform in life. The red sable is soft in texture and will retain elasticity; it's mostly used with watercolor or oil mediums, often for lettering. The red sable is the best—and most expensive—brush available. The Sabeline is a specially treated ox-hair, which is also used with watercolor or oil mediums, also for lettering. The bristle, which is obtained from boars or hogs, is a stiffer hair brush used with oil paints or tempera and for lettering. The camel-hair brush is derived from the Russian squirrel or pony hair; it's springy and can be used in a variety of ways, but its main purpose is for water-based mediums. The white synthetic fiber or Erminette is another all-purpose brush, which is very durable and is suggested for use with acrylics.

Brushes come in a wide variety of shapes and traditional names. Among them are bright, flat, fan, round, pointed, graphic arts, sky, bamboo, and showcard or lettering. For instance, the *bright* is flat with short hairs and a curved-in shape. It is used for most brushwork and brush techniques. The *flat* has longer hairs and is usually heavier than a bright. The flat is an excellent brush and produces a flexible stroke. The *sky* is a large, flat, oval brush with extremely long hairs that lend themselves to broad washes. Experiment with a variety of different shapes and sizes of brushes to find the one you are most comfortable with.

Palettes come in a variety of materials such as wood, plastic, and paper. I prefer the disposable types because they save time, and cleanup is effortless; you just throw them out when you are finished with them. For the water-based mediums, I use either an old china plate, a sheet of aluminum foil (mainly for acrylics), an aluminum circular pan, or a disposable plastic or paper palette. For oil paints and inks, I use a sheet of aluminum foil or a disposable paper palette.

I first dipped and removed most of the ink from my brush on scrap paper, and then worked on the dark areas in the coat and hat. When the brush became drier, I swung up in the face and neck areas to add the soft, drier brushstrokes.

The final drawing didn't have the feeling I wanted to convey—highlights weren't standing out. The areas I wanted to highlight were the man's sneering grin and his stark white shirt, which wasn't even dirtied as he killed the bull. The solution was to add a middle tone, so I used a very light purple pastel to highlight the white teeth and to separate the face from the white shirt.

Victory of the Matador
Waterproof India ink used with a no. 6 flat brush (light purple, soft pastel for touch up) drawn on High-Tech High-Surface Super Smooth illustration board

The drawing "Maine Landscape #2" was drawn with a no. 3 round brush, and the characteristics of the brush's stroke are clearly seen in the sketch. The thicker and heavier the stroke is the more pressure was applied to the brush, bending the brush hairs and causing more of the brush's surface to hit the paper. This particular sketch took most of an afternoon to complete because of the heavy amounts of ink that were applied and the great number of periodic breaks for drying time that were necessary so I would not smear ink.

Maine Landscape #2
India ink used with a no. 3 round brush, drawn on Morilla artist's bristol pad #188

I did the illustration above as an experiment, to see what kinds of strokes I could achieve in ink using only a wide, flat watercolor brush. I didn't plan the painting at all; its graphic shapes took form as the brush was tested. I worked the entire painting from light to dark, applying wet brushstrokes to the dry watercolor paper; I never dampened the watercolor paper before applying the ink.

Halfway through the testing of the brush, the landscape forms began to take shape, and I made an effort to formulate the random wet abstract brushstrokes into a recognizable picture. After the brushstrokes of the painting were completed and thoroughly dry, I added dark splash strokes for a spontaneous feel and additional variety. After the splash marks had dried, I used a

#3 technical pen and straightedge to add interesting lines that suggest tree trunks and planes of the earth in the landscape.

I used watercolor paper for this experiment because I thought its fast drying properties and very light texture would add to the light and middle tonal ranges of the ink.

Then I did another illustration, shown right, to take it one step further—to try to remove some of the paint from the paper's surface and have one to compare with the other.

When the second painting was complete, I conducted one final experiment. I dipped the same watercolor brush into clear water and applied it to highlight selective spots of the painting. I waited about eight seconds for the

water to penetrate and slightly dissolve the dried medium on the paper's surface, blotted the excess water from the area with a piece of wadded tissue paper, then very gently rubbed the area with a dry tissue to remove the medium from the paper surface. This lightened certain areas of the painting, mainly the darker tree areas. Because the trees were against or in front of a medium-tone value, highlighting them gave me an additional lighter tone to bounce against the dark tone. It created a light-dark-light tone range—a light tree in front of a darker tree against a light or medium tone background.

I not only learned from

this experiment about the brushstrokes, but also how watercolor paper reacts. For further experiments with this clear-water, medium-removal technique, I would use a much harder paper surface. The watercolor paper absorbed too much of the medium, and only a portion of the medium dried on the paper's surface. Using a paper with a harder surface, such as a bristol board or an illustration board, would give me better results, because most, if not all, of the applied medium would be deposited on the paper's surface. This would be much easier to rework and remove with the clear-water applications.

PRESNALL © 79

New Hampshire Landscapes
*Flat and round brushes and
nonwaterproof India ink drawn
on cold-press watercolor paper*

First I carefully planned this illustration and lightly sketched it out with a soft graphite pencil. Then I slowly built up the facial features of both men with the dry brush to achieve the desired darkness. This reworking and darkening procedure was carried out through the entire drawing, from start to finish. You can see that some of the lines in the young man's hat brim have been reworked and gone over to correct its oval shape. It's best, though, to keep the reworking (which leads to a darker area or line) to a minimum. The dry-brush technique should look fresh and easily rendered rather than dark and over-worked.

I needed plenty of extra scrap paper to do an illustration this large in dry brush. Every time I reinked my brush, I worked out some of the excess ink on scrap paper to give me a sufficiently dry brush.

I used a no. 6 round Grumbacher 1271 bristle oil brush to do this drawing. The bristles are obtained from boars or hogs—they're strong, very firm, and hold their shape nicely, wet or dry.

After the illustration was complete, I gently erased the sketched graphite line with a kneaded rubber eraser.

Sharing Music
Waterproof India ink, dry brush, drawn on Strathmore white linen paper

Although art critics may raise an eyebrow when they hear the words "finger painting," artists working in many different mediums use their fingers frequently to achieve a desired effect. In monotypes or drawings, for example, fingers are very useful to apply ink or to soften crosshatching. Art restorers have found Leonardo da Vinci's own fingerprints in the paint of some of his paintings. So don't hesitate to use your finger as a brush! The dramatic effects I achieved in these illustrations show that you can get both a bold line, from a well-inked finger, and a more feathery stroke, from an almost dry finger.

Untitled Finger Painted Sketches of Young Men
Drawn with my index finger dipped into a bottle of waterproof India ink and applied to plate-finish Morilla artist's bristol board

Finger Painting

Be creative with India ink. Virtually anything that has a point can be used to draw with. I did these drawings by dipping my fingertip in the ink, and finger painting.

The idea of using my finger to draw these came out of necessity. I wanted a large, thick line, as bold as I could get it. I have one of "those" brushes in the drawer—you know, the ones you never use and are always bumping into; a heavy, round brush, about one-half inch in diameter. I thought it would be ideal. But when I dipped it into my bottle of India ink, the brush sucked up the ink and emptied the entire bottle! As soon as I removed the brush from the bottle, the ink began dripping uncontrollably, and of course, as these things usually happen, I hadn't changed my clothes from a previous meeting, and my new, first-time-ever-worn pair of corduroy pants were ruined. Needless to say, I was a little upset. I realized I should have tried the brush with a little less ink, but it had already cost me a pair of pants, and I wasn't going to give it a second chance at my shirt! I threw it away, stuck my finger in another, full bottle of ink and started in.

I used plate-finish, Morilla artist's bristol board because the ink would dry mostly on the surface of this hard, smooth-finished board, and the paper's absorption would be kept to a minimum. Plus, the thickness of the board would prevent the wrinkling that occurs when ink is applied to paper.

Ink Washes

This is probably the most widely used wet-wash technique; it's by far the easiest. Surprisingly, both waterproof and nonwaterproof India inks can be used. When applied wet, both will produce a full scale of gray tones, but once the waterproof ink washes have fully dried, you can't rework them. What you see is what you get. But when you plan to combine an ink line with other water-based mediums (acrylic, dyes, or watercolor), use waterproof ink, so its line won't be lost or washed away, as may happen with the nonwaterproof ink.

Using your brush, mix the India ink and clear water in a separate tray or container and apply the tone to the paper. For lighter areas add more water; darker areas will need a higher proportion of ink. Use a heavier paper to reduce the chances of the paper buckling severely.

The drying time for the diluted ink washes will be long. You'll need to be patient; this time can be wisely spent in planning the next illustration step. The drying time may vary depending on the type of paper used, the amount of water and wash applied to the paper, and the atmospheric moisture or humidity. On rainy days when the humidity is 90 or 100 percent, the ink washes may take several hours to thoroughly dry. You can shorten the drying time by using a blow dryer.

On the Maine Coast
Nonwaterproof India ink drawn on High-Tech High Surface Super Smooth illustration board

The main difference between this illustration and "Western Union Line Men," opposite, is the paper. In fact, this really isn't paper—it's heavy illustration board. Although I used the same variety of brushes and worked from the top down on both illustrations, "On the Maine Coast" had no saturated wash areas. Because this paper is hard and smooth, its absorption rate is much less than that of watercolor paper, so the medium tends to dry on the surface. Another subtle difference is that I used an opaque white gouache to highlight areas of this illustration.

For "Western Union Line Men" I first sketched out the drawing, then saturated the area above the heads with clear water. While the paper was still very wet I applied diluted ink and watched the tone bleed into the water-saturated areas. After this area had dried completely, I continued working down the illustration. I added the dark background to help determine the lighter tones in the face and clothing areas. When those areas were completely dry, I added the ground spatterings, starting with light tones and gradually working up to darker tones. I used a tissue to immediately pick up any spatterings that fell in areas where I didn't want them. Finally, I added the sign in the upper right for balance.

Western Union Line Men
Nonwaterproof India ink drawn on Fabriano medium surface watercolor paper

This illustration started as a simple charcoal pencil drawing, for which I innocently chose a Strathmore drawing paper. After I'd completed the charcoal drawing and sprayed it lightly with workable fixative, I studied it for a while and decided to take it one step further. With a wide watercolor brush, I completely covered the drawing with a diluted nonwaterproof India ink wash to create a tone ground over the drawing. But after the wash was complete and as the drawing paper dried, it began to wrinkle and buckle. If paper dries severely wrinkled, it will never lay flat for eventual matting and framing, so I grabbed a roll of masking tape and a large wooden drawing board and frantically began to tape all the sides and corners of the paper to the drawing board. The tension on the taped paper had to be just right—too tight and the damp paper might tear, too loose and the wrinkles wouldn't be removed. I placed the board flat on the floor in the corner of my studio to dry as slowly as possible. Then I went to lunch.

Two hours later I returned to find the drawing had dried relatively flat with very little wrinkling. I'd saved the picture and was ready to dive into it again. I added a darker ink wash to pop the figure out just a little, and to give the drawing more depth. Again, I gave the drawing plenty of drying time (about half an hour). Then since I already had nice dark and medium tones in the picture, I figured I might as well add the

lighter ones now. Using an old china plate I mixed some Pro White and water to create a light opaque wash. I brushed this light wash in the background to highlight the figure's hair, bodice, and ruffled sleeves. After this wash had had plenty of time to dry, I carefully untaped the drawing and removed it from the drawing board.

Next, I wanted to visually soften the connection between the dark and light areas in the background, to accent the drawing with a repeated pattern. I ran out and bought a box of regular wooden (no. 2) writing pencils, with the yellow bodies and the pink rubber erasers on the end. Voilá!! The erasers provided a rubber stamp surface, and the pencil body provided a handle. To make a flower design cutout of the pencil eraser, I put a hole in the center of the eraser by twirling a small drill bit into it with my fingers. To cut the petals of the flower, I used my sharp penknife and carefully cut radiating lines into the eraser. I used a more opaque Pro White wash to test the stamp. I discovered the eraser would hold only enough Pro White for one print. A second stamp created another background shape and the buttons on the figure's dress. White pastel was added to suggest the outline of the couch and create highlights.

As the Day Grows Older
"BBB" Wolff's charcoal pencil with nonwaterproof India ink, Pro White paint and white pastel, drawn on Concept 900 heavy vellum paper

Stretching Your Paper

To stretch or not to stretch your paper is a question you must ask yourself when planning large wash areas. Watercolor papers should at times be stretched to minimize the severe wrinkling and buckling these heavy wash areas can cause. It's difficult, if not impossible, to mat and frame a piece of buckled paper, because it won't lay flat. Stretching will help the paper dry flat because the paper has been taped flat to a surface on all sides. To stretch your paper, you'll need the following supplies: a large wooden drawing board, a sponge, clear water, the watercolor paper, and a good supply of glued, paper tape. (Cellophane tape won't stick to wet paper, and paper tape has a slight stretching—or slight shrinking or pulling effect—on the paper as it dries.)

First, dampen the paper on both sides using the sponge. Next, cut four strips of the paper tape larger than the sides of the sheet of paper. Moisten the paper tape and apply the tape to the edges of paper and the wooden drawing board so the paper is securely taped to the board. As the tape and paper dry, the tape must be periodically checked to make sure it is secure to both the paper and board. Allow the damp paper to dry slowly and naturally; don't use a blow dryer or the paper may split. When stretching prestretched paper, you may encounter some wrinkling, but this should flatten out as it dries.

When the paper is dry, it's ready for the ink wash. I usually leave it taped to the board for my wash applications, because it seems to dry flatter. The paper may be removed from the board by cutting its edges with a razor blade.

First I drew this illustration on coarse newsprint with a crow quill pen and waterproof India ink. Then when the ink line was completely dry, I turned the drawing over and sprayed 3M 77 spray adhesive on the back; then I mounted it on a sheet of heavy illustration board to prevent the newsprint from wrinkling when I applied the wet, waterproof India ink washes. After it was securely mounted, I applied the washes with a wide, flat watercolor brush.

Three Rabbits
Waterproof India ink and crow quill line with a waterproof India ink wash, drawn on coarse newsprint

Mounting Your Paper

Mounting paper, like stretching paper, is done to prevent wrinkling. Mounting adds thickness and strength to thinner papers and can be done either before, during, or after the drawing is completed, just as long as the paper is dry and not already wrinkled. It's impossible to flatten out and mount a piece of wrinkled paper.

All types of paper can be mounted. It's an easy process, but proper ventilation and caution should be used when using spray adhesive! It can cause irreparable lung damage if inhaled over a period of time; that's why I use spray adhesive outside on the driveway with my artwork on a protective piece of cardboard. Then I bring the artwork back inside to mount. (I do this in winter, too.)

There are two types of spray adhesive: permanent and nonpermanent. Use the permanent-bond type. Permanent spray adhesive lets you mount the paper immediately after spraying, while the adhesive is still wet, or after it's thoroughly dry.

Once your sheet of paper is sufficiently sprayed, carefully place it on the board and gently pat it into place with your fingertips. Then put a sheet of tracing paper larger in size than the paper you're mounting over the mounted sheet (an inch or two of extra tracing paper all around is adequate). The tracing paper will protect the surface of the drawing paper while you're burnishing it. Now, while holding the tracing paper down with one hand, use the flat part of a fingernail on the other hand to rub and burnish the entire sprayed sheet, bonding it tightly to the heavy board surface. Remove the tracing paper, and voilà! One note of caution, allow enough time for the adhesive to thoroughly dry between your paper and board before proceeding with your wash.

My intended use of this sheet of paper wasn't for rendering a Surrealistic landscape but that accidentally took place. This sheet was used as a palette to mix both water and ink on, because I was outside sketching trees. I decided to add a wash to my sketch and took off for the brook for water. I mixed and used the wash from the paper, and when I had finished using it, laid it next to me in the hot sun and forgot about it. Later, I noticed the water had dried in two distinct puddles on the paper, which resembled the shape of trees. Reaching into my sketch travel kit, I grabbed a one-inch-long piece of graphite drawing stick, placed it on the paper, and dragged it along the surface of the paper to indicate a simplified, toned background. I interrupted this background tone line with white spaces near the base of the tree wash, where the trunk would be located, so when I added in the trunk of the tree, it would be highlighted and not get lost in the background tone. The shadows on the ground, under the trees are simply indicated with the outlines of the oval shapes they made.

One note: the sketch paper's tooth is nicely shown and accentuated by the graphite drawing stick line.

Landscape Profile
Ink wash with "B" graphite drawing stick drawn on Strathmore sketch paper

I planned this illustration and chose a paper that would hold up under the stress of several wash applications. Then, using a wide, flat watercolor brush and several different diluted waterproof India ink washes, I started with a series of varied tonal, graphic, outline shapes of the tree, its main trunk, and the ground surface. Since this was going to be an abstract of a banyan tree, I was mainly concerned with shapes and their relationships rather than dimension. I allowed plenty of drying time (about twenty minutes) between each of the tone wash applications, that is, I never applied them wet on wet.

Then I turned the painting upside down and, holding the same brush by the end of its long handle, swung the brush several times in the air to make spatter marks to indicate individual leaves.

Next I added the background tone areas and the tone inside the tree. When this had completely dried, I made darker spatter marks inside and outside the tree areas and added a tonal shadow band at the bottom of the tree to create the illusion of a background landscape. The next step was to use the same brush and the ink directly from the bottle to create the black descriptive outline shapes of the tree, its main trunk, and the ground surface. To draw in the tree branches, limbs, and connecting roots, I chose a #2 technical pen and a straightedge for the consistent, dark lines they would render. These lines helped define the spatter marks as an interesting and important part of the picture, which not only contributed to the overall upward movement of the tree, but added the detail of individual leaves.

Portrait of a Tree, #2 Waterproof India ink and #2 technical pen line and flat brush with a waterproof India ink wash, drawn on plate-finish, illustration board

Clear Water Wash

I purposely touched the felt-tip lines in this drawing with a wet sable brush so the lines would dissolve and bleed in the dampened area. I didn't bother to clean out the brush but continued to wash the areas with clear water; only after I'd completed the illustration did I thoroughly rinse the brush. Once the wash was complete, I didn't rework or redraw the pen line.

Carousel Cowboy
Pilot Razor Point pen and clear water, drawn on plate-finish bristol board

The clear water wash technique uses water and a water-soluble medium—watercolor, dye, nonpermanent water-based felt-tip, or nonwaterproof India ink—to produce soft tonal areas. The clear water is washed over the drawn line, which then spreads or bleeds to produce subtle, imaginative, sometimes visually explosive tonal areas.

This technique is spontaneous and really fun to do. Part of its beauty is that you really don't know what you're going to end up with. The clear water wash isn't that easy to see when it's applied, and the shade of the tone it picks up will be slightly lighter when it dries.

After you've completed your line drawing, wet a clean brush and apply it to the area you wish to tone; the ink or water-soluble medium you used for drawing will mix with the water and produce the tone. Since the tone's darkness is determined by the amount of ink used in the drawing process, you'll need more ink for dark tonal areas. These areas may have to be worked and reworked with both additional ink and clear water. On the other hand, if you find you've got too much tone, let it dry, then apply more clear water to "wash" the tone; pick up the tone by blotting it with a rag or tissue.

Some daring artists may first completely dampen or soak the whole sheet of paper before drawing on it. Again, using a water-soluble drawing medium, they draw on the paper as it dries. The wet and dry areas on the paper produce different types of lines. This technique is more explosive than the applied wash technique, because you can't control the line being drawn on a wet piece of paper.

As in "Carousel Cowboy," I drew this illustration with a black, water-soluble, Pilot Razor Point pen. This time I selected a no. 6 red sable brush because it would hold much more water for the larger wash areas I wanted in this drawing. As I worked the illustration with a very wet wash, I brushed water on liberally, allowing it to touch and dissolve, or in some cases completely erase, the drawn pen line. In some of the wash areas, especially where the figure's line meets the wash, the bleeding of the line into the wash is noticeable. All the tones in this illustration came from the previously drawn pen lines.

After the wash had completely dried, I again used the felt-tip to touch up or redraw those lines the wash had erased, especially around the outline of the figure.

The Harvest
Felt-tip pen and clear water, drawn on Hammermill bond paper

Scratchboard

After I sketched this on scratchboard, I outlined all the forms with a Hunt #112 scratch knife. I chose that blade because of its very sharp tip and straight razor edge, which gave me a sharp white line. I then switched to a Hunt #113 with its curved razor edge to remove the large background areas. Then I switched back to the #112, and using a straightedge, scratched the four edges to frame in the drawing. I finished with the #113 and a small, thin brush and ink for touch-up work.

Magic Art
Scratchboard worked with Hunt scratch knives #112 and #113

Scratchboard could perhaps qualify as a medium, but since it dictates technique I've included it in Part Two. Scratchboard is just a white cardboard sheet coated with heavy white clay. A light layer of India ink is then brushed on, which dries only on the clay's surface. The artist lightly scratches the black ink-coated surface off to reveal the white clay.

Scratchboard comes in different weights—12-point board or premounted on 90-point board—and in both prepared (the ink surface already on) and unprepared varieties. Your purpose and design will help determine which you choose. For example, if your design has a black background or many dark areas, the prepared surface is your best choice. But for a drawing with a white background or many light areas, you'd be better off using the unprepared surface to sidestep the tedious job of removing large areas of the black scratchboard surface. As you work the drawing, you can brush the ink only in those areas you wish to make dark.

Just about anything can be used as a scratching tool, a pin, a knife, a single edge razor blade—you can make the tool yourself. There are many different inexpensive scratch tools available at art supply stores. Scratchboard tools are small knives about the size of pen tips. These knife points have bodies that closely resemble lettering and drawing pens and will fit into pen holders for easy handling. Lithographic points are available for "drawing" on scratchboard; there are also multiliner scratch tools with multiple points for drawing several parallel lines at once. These are useful for crosshatching.

The blade edge and point of scratching tools must be kept sharp to produce the best possible line. If the blade or point becomes dull, a fine oil stone (or wet stone) should be used for sharpening.

My scratchboard tools consist mainly of two scratch knives and a large diaper pin. The first knife is my all-purpose knife, a Hunt scratch knife No. 112. It has a triangular shaped blade and is great for scratching fine lines. The second knife is a Hunt scratch knife No. 113. It has a point that makes fine scratch lines and a curved edge for broader lines. I use the sharp point of the diaper pin to produce very fine scratch lines.

Experiment with different types of tools to see what effects you can achieve, but use only light pressure to remove the ink from the surface. You don't need to remove all the clay on the board surface—in fact, this is a bad idea because the underlying white clay is what gives the scratched line its sharp edge. The clay also adds strength to the board; in other words, if you were to gouge away all of the clay down to the paper's surface this would weaken the higher clay and ink ridges left behind. Any accidental rubbing or bumping of the board could chip or break off these higher ridges.

One distinct advantage of scratchboard is that mistakes can very easily be corrected simply by brushing on more ink. Wait until the newly applied ink is completely dry and then you can rework the area. If the ink isn't dry and you continue to work, you'll get an undesirable blurred effect. The scratched lines on the board should be crisp and clear. As a general rule, always keep scratchboard in a dry place and make sure the board is completely dry before using it.

This illustration uses large contrasting areas of white and black; details are kept to a minimum, suggesting a silhouette in design and look. (The silhouette style is covered on page 146.) I used a prepared (pre-inked) scratchboard and Hunt #112 and #113 scratch knives. I used the sharp, pointed #112 scratch knife to first sketch out the illustration, and later for fine line areas such as the grass. The sharp, beveled edge of the #113 scratch knife (which incidentally fit in a normal pen holder) was used to remove larger areas of the inked surface; the sky was quickly scratched away with one pass of the knife along the outer borders. Some of the scratched areas were later touched up, reworked, or corrected by reinking the surface with India ink and a small highlighter brush.

Landscape with Sheep
Essdee British pre-inked scratchboard worked with Hunt scratch knives #112 and #113

Acrylic Polymer Medium

Acrylic gel medium is a liquid polymer, water-soluble medium available in both crystal clear and matte finishes. Both types dry to a flexible, permanent finish. This polymer mixes well with all water-based mediums. In mixing, the amount of polymer, water, and ink will determine the tonal grade of the medium. Use less polymer for smoother tones, more polymer for interesting textured brush strokes. I would suggest using a separate sheet of paper to experiment with your mixture first before applying it to your final art. It's better at first to go lighter with your tones because they can be darkened later if need be. Polymer dries in a relatively short time, but you can add a special acrylic retarder to prolong the drying time.

All types of brushes can be used with polymer. An acrylic paintbrush is made of nylon fiber, but don't be swayed by "acrylic" on the label, experiment with all different kinds. (See page 74 for a discussion of brushes.)

In applying acrylic medium, try to use as few brushstrokes as possible since the brush molds the acrylic as it's applied to the paper. Vary your brushstrokes in direction, length, and speed. In the top left corner of the illustration "Good Friends," opposite, you can almost see from the brushstroke the speed with which it was applied.

After using any kind of acrylic medium, wash your brush thoroughly with a mild soap-and-water solution. It's worthwhile to take your time and do a thorough cleaning, because if any of the polymer dries on the brush, you might as well take the brush into the backyard and bury it—it's ruined.

"Good Friends" started as a magazine short story illustration. The story takes place in the early 1920s and is about a boy whose grandfather loves to tell stories about his wife now deceased; all the man had to remind him of her beauty was an old photograph taken around 1890. One day, the boy and his grandfather posed together for their own photograph. Years later, after the boy grew into a man, he was looking through an old photo album and came upon both photos. He thought back about his childhood, the happiness and carefree days he had spent with his grandfather.

I wanted to visually tell the story with only an introduction illustration of the three family members. The technique I chose needed to reflect the time and fashion of the time, and have quality reproduction for the magazine. So I chose to use a combination of ink (for good crisp line reproduction) and acrylic gel medium to soften the illustration and add a little texture.

First I drew the India ink line. It was important to use waterproof India ink because later I would be working over the line art with a water-soluble medium. After the ink was dry, I cut thin strips of adhesive tape and mounted them on the art board vertically behind the grandfather, into the photograph to draw the eye to the boy's face and into the photograph. I also covered the white border around the photograph. Now the line art was ready for the acrylic gel medium. Using a no. 10 Grumbacher series 615 red sable brush, I mixed ink and acrylic and applied it across the tape, into the photograph, over the taped photo borders, and into the background area.

After the first light acrylic areas had dried, I carefully removed the tape, pulling it up slowly so as not to tear the paper. Using the same brush as before (which I'd thoroughly cleaned after the first use) I again mixed ink and polymer to a darker value and applied this to the corners of the photo, the grandmother's dress, the grandfather's suit and shoes, and the boy's stockings and shoes. Then I again thoroughly cleaned my brush. To "pop" the grandmother out of the dark-value photograph area, I used a mixture of Pro White and acrylic gel to highlight various areas of the photo background.

Good Friends
Waterproof India ink and #1
technical pen line with a
waterproof India ink and gel
medium wash, drawn on Pentalic
Paper for Pens

First this illustration was sketched out with a soft graphite pencil; then all the lines—with the exception of the circle lines of the wheels—were inked over with waterproof India ink in a #00 technical pen. A compass with an adaptable stainless steel pen attached to it was used to make the large pen line circles for the tires. These pens can be very tricky to use, and for the best possible results the pen should be very clean.

The compass pen is adjustable, which means its point can be changed from very thin to heavy line thicknesses. The heavier lines are dangerous to make because since the ink is gravity fed, it may flow too quickly off the tip—and you end up with a blob the size of Milwaukee on your drawing paper (my apologies to Milwaukee). So I adjusted the compass pen to a very thin line setting to match the technical pen line width and added just a little ink. (Never overload the pen, you can always add more ink, but you can't do much about a big glob of ink.)

I placed the pointed end of the compass in the center point of the wheel and made one complete smooth, sweeping motion to form the outer round line of the tire. Keeping the compass point stationary, I adjusted the center wheel on the compass to bring the pen point closer to the center point and inked another circular tire line. This procedure was repeated until the tire was finished.

Now, to get both tire measurements and line distances identical, I removed the pen point assembly from the compass and replaced it with the pencil point assembly, then took the time to clean all of the ink off of the pen point. I used the compass and pencil to measure the first tire and then mark the second in the foreground pair, then again in the background pair. Each time, after the second tire was marked with graphite, I switched back to the pen point assembly to complete the tire.

I used a kneaded eraser to gently remove all the graphite lines of my original sketch. I kept the background simple (empty) so as not to distract from the foreground. I oversimplified the spokes in the tires to avoid driving myself crazy drawing in all the insignificant tire spoke detail; also, by leaving the inside of the tire areas blank, I left it up to the viewer to decide whether or not the vehicle was moving or standing still.

All the tones in the illustration were created by mixing waterproof India ink with acrylic gel medium and applied with round red sable brushes. I established the lighter tones first, and added more gel medium as I went along with the darker tones. I used Pro White to pop the wheel spokes out of the acrylic toned areas, and a thin mixture of Pro White and acrylic gel medium was used to highlight Ford's hat, coat, and pants.

H. Ford
Waterproof India ink and #00 technical pen line with a waterproof India ink and acrylic gel medium wash, drawn on 2 ply, plate-finish bristol board

Aerosol

A full can of paint creates a finely grained coverage.

A can that's three quarters full produces a slightly coarser, spattering-type coverage.

A half-full can renders much coarser, and darker, coverage.

An aerosol that's one-quarter full results in very coarse, sporadic coverage.

You can create a variety of textural effects by having at hand four cans of enamel spray paint with varying amounts of paint and aerosol in each. As you can see above, textures that can be achieved range from very fine to very coarse and spatter-like. Also note the differences in tone from sample to sample.

This technique uses paper stencils and ordinary enamel spray paint. The paper stencil is cut, placed on the base paper and sprayed with paint. The tone or darkness of an area is determined by the amount of paint and how it's applied. The beauty of this technique is that you can work from light to dark or vice versa. With this type of opaque enamel, white will nicely cover black.

Stencils can be carefully planned or used spontaneously. To plan a stencil, first pencil out your entire drawing. Then tape a large sheet of heavy, clear acetate over the base drawing to protect it from being cut. Now, tape the paper to be used as the stencil over the acetate sheet. You can use almost any type of paper for a stencil; I generally use bond paper. Place the three sheets on a light table; you should be able to clearly see the base drawing through the stencil paper. Your base drawing will remain intact beneath the acetate and can be used to cut all the stencils you need.

When cutting stencils, use a very sharp knife and apply only enough pressure to cut through the stencil paper and *not* through the acetate. Once the stencil is cut, carefully remove it from the acetate sheet and put it on the paper you intend to use for your art. When you're ready to cut the next stencil, simply tape another clean sheet of paper over the acetate and repeat the tracing process.

To use stencils spontaneously, you simply place them on a sheet of paper and spray around them, let the paint dry, then move them around and spray again. Try a variety of shapes and sizes of stencils. The background tones you create will act as a ground for the lighter and darker tones to be

added later. At times, if I have a basic idea for an illustration, I'll purposely begin the illustration with this random spraying of different shapes and forms from paper stencils for a spontaneous and creative background. Once the background is finished, I can spray either lighter or darker tones or colors over the background.

I'll sometimes use three or four different cans of the same color paint on a single illustration. A new can with plenty of aerosol will usually produce a very fine spray, but as the can empties and the aerosol is used up, it creates a spattering effect. I use three or four cans for various effects: a full can, a can three-quarters full, another half full, and another one-quarter full. For example, a light burst of spray from a full can of black paint will produce a fine gray area, whereas a one-quarter-filled can creates a spattered effect.

In general, very light sprays are best. Use short bursts of the spray enamel at a distance of about two feet from the final art board. Short bursts will allow you to continually check the tone of the area being worked on.

On fine-detailed areas, where the stencil is very small, a little dab of rubber cement may be applied to the stencil to hold it in place on the final art board. This prevents the stencil from blowing off the board, and believe me, some of the aerosol cans can be very windy, especially if they are new cans.

Take all necessary precautions while using spray enamel paint. Use it only in a well-ventilated room and wear a mask over your nose and mouth.

Once you've finished spraying the

paint, allow ample time for it to dry before removing the stencil, or you're liable to smear the wet paint. Drying time depends on the type of paint and the amount that is sprayed on. Heavier coats will take longer to dry, but the average coat will take ten to twenty minutes to dry thoroughly. New types of spray enamel labeled "fast drying" may only take a few minutes to dry. Testing the paint for dryness is easily done by lightly touching the excess paint on the stencil with the tip of the finger.

This painting uses several stencils and was great fun to put together. The skipper, standing on the boat in the foreground, is the official judge of the boat race. The detail is kept mainly in the foreground, boat and water areas, and the background is left simple and suggestive, with only the boat and sail shapes to define the horizon.

Hard to Judge
Enamel spray paint and stencils on 2 ply, plate-finish bristol board

97

This illustration started as an experiment with tone and highlight. I wanted to see if just a medium tone, a light tone, and highlights could successfully make an illustration work, devoid of any dark or strong black areas. I wanted to make the highlights tell the whole story.

First I cut a large stencil for the entire shape of the colored background area; I sprayed this area with a new can of gray enamel paint, then, with an almost empty can of black spray paint for the spattered effect. To make the can spatter even more, I used short, one-quarter-second bursts. I removed the stencil when the paint was thoroughly dry and the background tone ground was complete. Next, I cut a stencil for the car and placed it in position on the tone ground, sprayed surface. In the finer detail areas where the stencil pieces were tiny, such as the tire tread, hubs, and headlights, I put a dab of rubber cement on the stencil pieces to keep them in place on the painted surface. After the car stencil was in position I sprayed it lightly with white enamel paint. When it was thoroughly dry, each piece of the car stencil was carefully removed. Last, a stencil for the two horns was cut (in the center of a large piece of paper), placed in position, and lightly sprayed with a light gray enamel paint. When the last stencil was thoroughly dry it was carefully removed.

The Chicago Get Away Car
Enamel spray paint and stencils, on illustration board

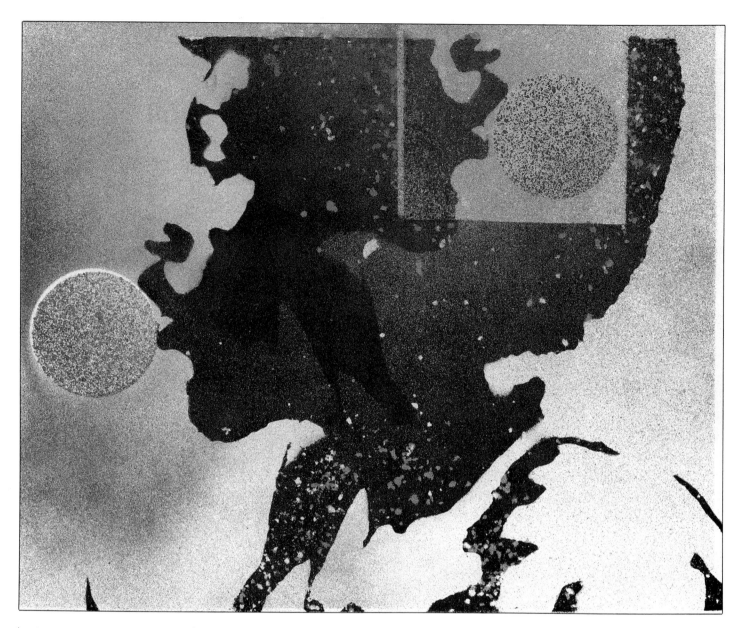

This illustration was fun to do—I got the idea while showing my daughter how to blow bubbles with bubble gum. While I was slowly blowing up the bubble and keeping a sharp eye on it at the same time, I realized that I could only see the top part, yet, my mind's eye could clearly calculate its entire size. I wanted to illustrate this concept.

First, I cut a large rectangular paper stencil and placed it on a large sheet of bristol board. The entire illustration would appear in this area. After figuring out where the bubble was to be placed, I placed a smaller, circular stencil on the board.

Next I sprayed a light gray tone ground on the entire illustration. When this dried, I removed both stencils from the board, and replaced these with the large paper stencil of the head and shoulders (with a blocked rectangular section in the back of the head). I sprinkled a few tiny pebbles inside the stencil, around the head, neck, and shoulders. I sprayed it with a very light coat of gray paint. When the paint had dried, I sprinkled a few more pebbles and applied a coating of black spray paint. I allowed the paint to dry, then removed all the stencils and pebbles.

The facial paper stencil was flopped and repositioned in the back of the head area to work on the mind's eye area. I added a light coat of black spray paint to produce the nose, mouth, and chin in the mind's eye area.

To add a little interest, I flopped the other, positive, part of the stencil (produced when the stencil was cut out) and placed it on the board over the black area. I matched it up with the chin, mouth, and nose in the mind's eye area. I sprayed a short burst of white paint.

Then I found the other part of the bubble stencil, placed it on the left side of the board, and gave it a short, spatter burst of black. Finally, I repositioned the same stencil in the mind's eye area and gave it a short burst.

Bubble Blowing in the Mind's Eye
Enamel spray paint and stencils, on 2 ply, plate-finish bristol board

I worked this illustration from the top down. The large dark rectangular shape was sprayed in first to act as a tone ground. The bubbles were created by using a can of paint set on the paper as a stencil. For the woman's face, I cut a paper stencil. (Since I was using white spray enamel to highlight the face, this meant anything that I intended to be dark in the face, such as the eyes or mouth, would be covered by the paper stencil.) I put tiny dabs of rubber cement on the back of the stencil pieces so the aerosol "wind" wouldn't blow them out of place. Removing the stencil of the woman's face, I then placed successive stencils for the connecting center bar, the workmen, and the foreground area. For the latter, I rubber cemented thin strips of paper to the painting to graphically add a pile of strewn railroad rails and ties on the ground. Then I dropped cat litter and very fine pebbles on this area before spraying with black enamel to add the look of some rocky soil. Remember, very light sprays are recommended, you can always build up and darken an area.

Looking over the nearly completed illustration, I felt I needed to somehow graphically tie in the woman's face with the workmen. To do this I added thought bubbles to one of the workers by cutting a hole in a large sheet of paper leaving a lot of excess paper surrounding the cutout circle to protect the rest of the illustration.

As you plan the stencils and cut them out of the paper be aware of how and where the stencil is go-ing to be used. With a small amount of rubber cement, three of the thin paper stripes used for the railroad track rails were pasted directly on the finished art. This gave me the ability to move the circle stencil around several times and still keep the three pasted vertical stripes of paper in place. For the last bubble (far left) the circle stencil was positioned and then, to add visual texture, cat litter was sprinkled on.

Railroad Guardian Angel
Enamel spray paint and stencils, on illustration board

Duo-Shade Board

Here you can see the two tones created using Duo-Shade board and developers #1 and #2.

Rubber Ducky
Drawn and stylized in waterproof India ink with a #1 technical pen and french curve on Grafix Duo-Shade #265 board

Duo-Shade board is bristol board with two, invisible light- and dark-pattern screens printed on its surface. These screens instantly appear when tone developers are brushed on. You use two tone developers: one to produce the light shade pattern and another to produce the dark. The sequence in which the tone developer is applied doesn't matter, you can go from light to dark or vice versa.

Duo-Shade board is widely used by cartoonists and fashion illustrators and is available in many different tone and shade patterns such as stipple and crosshatch, and in seven or eight different screen values, fine to coarse.

Duo-Shade bristol board will accept almost any medium, although ink, felt tip, and charcoal (for fashion illustrations) are most often used. I always use waterproof ink—I certainly wouldn't want to run the risk of the developers' causing my water-based-ink lines to run, thus ruining an entire finished drawing. You'll need both developers: #1, light tone developer, and #2, dark tone developer. They're usually sold separately from the boards, so don't forget them!

It's important never to mix the tone developers when they are wet, so you'll need separate brushes for each of the developers. I used to have trouble remembering which brush was which, so now I just tape a piece of masking tape around the end of the handle and identify each as #1 or #2. You'll also need a blotter.

After you've sketched your drawing on the Duo-Shade board, it's time for the magic. Dip your brush in a developer and brush it on, then blot the board to pick up any excess developer. Always use a clean, dry portion of your blotter (I use a tissue or blotter paper) to pick up the excess developer, or you might touch an area you don't want developed with the wet blotter, and lo and behold, it will become developed.

Planning the shading is important. It is easy to transfer from light to dark, dark to light, but once it's developed, it cannot be erased. Most of the time, I will first finish the line drawing and then use developer #1 throughout the entire drawing. Then I will use developer #2 to finish the drawing. This is easier because sometimes developer #1 will dictate the areas where developer #2 should be used.

Many art supply stores don't stock Duo-Shade board, although they're often happy to order it for you, so call around before you rush across town to buy it.

First the illustration was drawn out in felt-tip. Then I applied light-tone developer #1 to establish the middle tone areas. I added dark-tone developer #2 to finish the illustration. (The developers were applied with separate #10 red sable brushes.) Finally, I used Pro White to highlight a few spots on the eyebrow and on the catcher's mitt and shin guards.

Baseball Catcher
Drawn with a Pilot Razor Point felt-tip on Grafix Duo-Shade

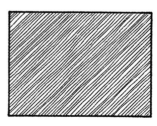

**Light Tone
Developer #1**

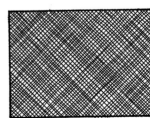

**Dark Tone
Developer #2**

Montage

A montage combines several pictures or drawings into one. The montage is two-dimensional, as opposed to collage and assemblage, which are three-dimensional. Because a montage is made up of diverse elements, balance and proportion play important roles in its composition—without them it may look jumbled. Different subjects and techniques may be successfully integrated to render a montage illustration, but the montage technique is mostly used to show a story and its principal parts in one picture. The classic examples are book covers or movie posters, which may picture several characters' faces, a setting or two, and other subjects such as a weapon, a car, a rose, a crucifix, and so on.

Often in designing the combination of montage elements, I'll create a negative space or area where the next element can gracefully fit. These negative, outlined areas are easily created with a series of parallel lines (vertical, horizontal, angular), circles, squares, rectangles, etc. You'll find these linear shapes and design elements in just about every montage illustration I've done. For example, in the montage of the BMW on the opposite page, the top illustration is surrounded by a linear, rectangular, negative area, which is purposely used to buffer the connection of the interior and the front-end view of the auto. Directly below the interior view, the square shape reappears in the shape of the sign, which abuts the flat, top, linear shape of the grill area.

Venus with Pelican, M. Waterproof India ink used with a #0 technical pen for line and stipple on Pentalic Paper for Pens

This illustration uses the same linear-designed, outlined, negative areas described in the text for connecting the important illustrated parts of the montage. These important areas are also visually separated because I used different illustration styles and techniques to draw them: the silhouette shape at the bottom, rising up to the stippling; then into the horizontal line style in the woman's hair and background, and then into the pelican, which employs stipple, line, and silhouette shadow. (The horizontal line style will be discussed in detail on page 136.)

This montage was designed to make the eye travel in a vertical direction. The viewer's eye will cover all the important parts if the montage is viewed either from top to bottom or vice versa.

Careful planning went into this montage. I took sizes, proportions, and vantage points into consideration while sketching and combining the elements; one big advantage I had with this particular montage was a good selection of reference photographs. The top illustration gives the overall view of the car; the next view, of the interior, is strategically placed to visually connect with the largest view of the car. This low view leads into the sign, which is immediately connected with an enlarged view of the auto' grill and headlight design.

Now take a look at the balance of the BMW montage illustration. For this you will need something long and narrow, like a new, wooden pencil. Place this book flat on a table, opened to this page. You are going to visually divide this BMW montage illustration in half using the pencil. Lay the pencil vertically on the illustration so the pencil lead lies in the middle of the car grill in the top illustration and the eraser lies on top of the left headlight in the bottom illustration. Notice that the illustration's weight is balanced when the montage is divided in half by the pencil: the large area on the left side of the largest illustration in the center, equally balances with the smaller illustration areas on the right side of the montage.

1938 BMW Model 328
Waterproof India ink with a #00 technical pen for line with a waterproof India ink wash on plate-finish bristol board

105

Collage

Collage in French means "pasting," and that makes sense because collages are composed of just about anything that can be pasted into place. Collage differs subtly from montage in that collage is three-dimensional. Whereas montage combines several pictures *on a flat surface,* collage elements (torn bits of paper, fabric, chickenwire, matchbook covers, etc.) are often actual *objects* which jut out from the paper. A collage can even be carried all the way to sculpture (what's known as an *assemblage*), but for our purposes here, we'll consider only the "slightly" three-dimensional ones.

My first collage was done at the ripe old age of six—maybe yours was too. I remember having a great time pasting all those different colored noodles, elbow macaroni, and glitter on a sheet of construction paper. I think there were also some toothpicks strewn around on the page . . . Does that ring a bell? But whether or not you've ever made a collage before, it's a fun technique to try. Collage can be combined or used in conjunction with other mediums—paint or ink, for instance—and the materials you use in a collage are limited only by your imagination. Collages may even have commercial as well as fine art uses, depending on the subject matter.

"Fish and Peas" uses cutup fish prints (see page 121 for instructions), silverware, and halftone block areas (for the checkered tablecloth) cut out of old magazines, all pasted on a sheet of bristol board. The peas were created by dipping the end of a new eraser on a #2 writing pencil in ink and stamping it several times on the paper, then outlining them using a technical pen and a circle template. The fun lies in the fact that some fishermen stuff and hang their prize fish on their walls—I've hung a picture collage of the end result on mine, which is a good meal!

Fish and Peas, which is better than Liver
Collage, pasted on 2 ply, plate bristol board

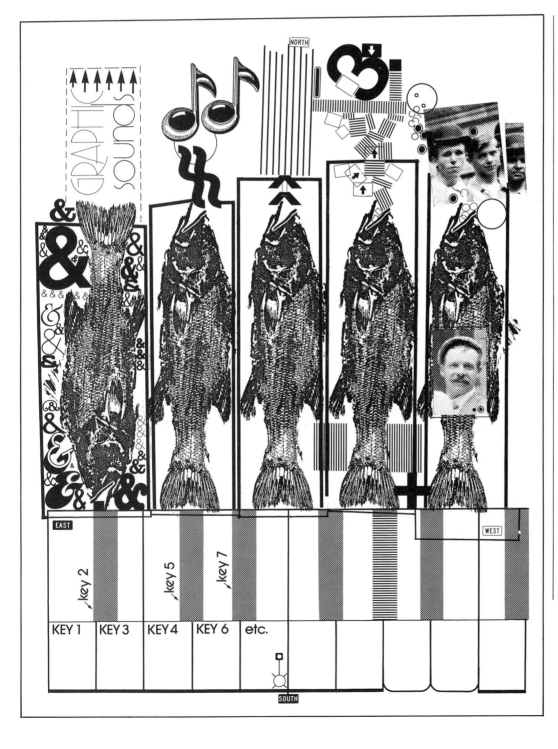

In this collage I combined several different flat objects to complete the picture. I used six of my fish monotypes (see page 121), printed halftone screens. I cut the ampersands and several other preprinted design shapes from several magazines and drew the musical notes, rules, circles, and arrows with a technical pen and India ink. All of the pasting was done with a spray adhesive.

"Fish Organ" came about as the result of an experiment to see if I could combine two views from different vantage points in the same illustration. The first view is the left side of an organ keyboard, looking directly down it. The second view represents a rectangular, cut-away view of the organ pipes where the music is made. But I designed it so the fish themselves are making the music, represented by the graphic shapes and drawn forms.

Fish Organ
Collage, pasted on 2 ply, plate-finish bristol board

Again the fish shows up in the graphic collage "Fish Kite," above. The clothes, hands, and tail of the kite were cutout halftone sections from a magazine, and the remaining parts of this collage were inked in with waterproof India ink and a #1 technical pen. It first was drawn out with a pencil. Then I placed it on a light table and placed another sheet of paper on top of it. On this sheet, I first pasted down the halftone areas, then inked in the areas that were drawn on the underlying sheet of paper.

Fish Kite
Collage, pasted on 2 ply, plate bristol board

Years ago when I was "paying my dues" to the art world while trying to sell my work in local art shows, I met a lot of people who wanted sofa-sized paintings to match their dark brown carpet and orange living room walls, all for two bucks. It's to these people I dedicate my collage "The Friday Night Boys," right, because I made it specially to hang in my dining room! The shirts of the three men in the picture are made of the actual wallpaper hanging in the dining room and pantry. And yes, this collage is in color, or maybe you thought I had black-and-white wallpaper?

It all started with an old photograph I'd purchased in a funky antique store in Harvard Square, Cambridge. I had it converted to a halftone (so the tones would appear as dots), and enlarged it to 950 percent, which is pretty big as enlargements go. I then taped this enlargement or "stat" to my light table and, with a #1 technical pen, traced and inked all of the black dot areas in the men (except within the shirt areas) onto the bristol board. Next, I took a piece of tracing paper and, using the light table, carefully traced each man's shirt. Then I turned the tracing paper over and rubbed a

soft, black graphite pencil over the drawn line on the other side of the tissue paper to create a crude form of carbon paper. I then took an extra piece of wallpaper, placed the carboned tissue paper over it (so the carboned side was against the patterned side of the wallpaper) and, by retracing over the lines on the tissue paper I had previously drawn, transferred the line from the tissue paper onto the wallpaper. I carefully cut this area out of the wallpaper with my penknife, sprayed the back of the wallpaper with spray adhesive, placed the wallpaper on the bristol board, and burnished it into place. The same procedure was followed for the other two shirts using two other wallpapers. Finally, I inked in the shadow areas in the center shirt in the collage and added the top left stripes.

The Friday Night Boys
Collage, pasted on 2 ply, plate bristol board

Wax Resist and Rubbings

A sample of a wax rubbing from a zinc printing plate with a black wax crayon.

The same art with a gray wash of diluted, waterproof India ink.

Wax will resist water, thus any water-based medium can be used to produce a wax resist drawing. Dye, ink, watercolor, tempera (opaque watercolor powder), and gouache would be fun to experiment with. If the line in the resist drawing is done in white wax (usually white paraffin or a very light-colored wax is used) the background area will accept the added medium (which is generally dark, for good contrast), while the waxed areas will remain white.

A wax rubbing, as its name implies, is a rubbing done with a piece of wax (usually a dark or black-colored wax, large enough to easily hold in the hand), which is rubbed on a thin piece of paper to capture the detail, texture, or any raised portion of the surface under the paper.

Rubbings are easy to do. First, make sure the paper is taped down securely over the object, pattern, or texture you are going to rub. If the paper moves or travels slightly in the rubbing process, you'll get a double image. Once the paper is secure, you're ready to apply the wax. For white wax, I use candles because they're easy to find, inexpensive, and thick enough to lend themselves to easy handling. For the black and darker colors and tones I use inexpensive crayons.

Wax application on rubbings depends on the patterns or textures that are being transferred to the paper. Sometimes, light, short, even strokes of the wax may work well. Other times, light, small, circular strokes may be what you need. Don't be afraid to experiment with the wax application strokes, but remember the wax shouldn't be thickly or heavily applied at first (that's why I specifically said "light" strokes). Your best bet is to slowly build up the darkness of the rubbing with layers of the light strokes.

Rubbings can easily be combined with a wax resist method. A dark-colored wax is usually used for the rubbing, with a lighter-colored water-based medium for the background. The combination of white wax on white paper is more difficult to use because obviously white on white is hard to see, so there's no way to check if your drawing or rubbing is complete. Also, be aware that the drawing may appear to be reversed, because it's a white line on a dark background.

Experiment with different types of paper to find the kind best suited to your needs. For wax resist with a water-based medium, a paper with a high absorption rate probably works best. A thin, good-quality paper with a hard, smooth or slick surface works better for wax rubbings: a white bond or a relatively smooth sketching paper. An easy rule to remember is, the thicker the paper, the less detail you will get from the object you are rubbing. If you wish to add a water wash resist to the rubbing, it's a good idea to mount the thinner sheet with the rubbing on it (use permanent spray adhesive) to a heavier sheet to minimize wrinkling. (Refer back to page 84 for details on mounting your paper.)

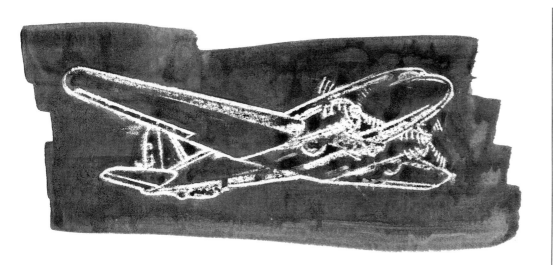

A sample of the wax resist method done with a white paraffin stick (candle) line on Strathmore series 300 sketch paper. I used a zinc printing plate to make the rubbing; the background wash is a diluted, water-proof India ink, applied with a wide brush.

The same wax rubbing done with a black wax crayon with an added texture background. The rubbing of the airplane was placed on a rough cement floor, and the paper was gently rubbed with the same crayon. The paper is Pentalic Paper for Pens.

Linoleum Cuts and Prints

Linoleum or lino printing is classified as a *relief transfer*. In carving and cutting the lino, the positive areas to be printed are left on the surface, while the negative areas are removed. Be aware that when the lino surface is printed, it will transfer in the opposite manner on the paper—what is being carved on the left side will actually print on the right side. For instance, if there is a message or lettering on the lino surface, you must carve out the letters backward, in reverse, so that when the type is printed on the paper it will read correctly. To check the design, hold the lino image in front of a mirror.

Lino blocks are available in most art supply stores. The lino thickness will range from one-eighth to one-quarter inch. The linoleum is usually mounted on a plywood base. Linos produce crisp, sharp edges for your illustration or design purposes.

To start, if you have a design or illustration already drawn on paper, you may transfer the drawing to the lino with regular typewriter carbon paper. Or you can make your own graphite paper by simply turning the drawing over and scumbling a soft, dark graphite (I like to use an Ebony pencil) over the sheet. Place the carbon or graphited paper face down on the lino block, put your sketch or design on top, then trace the lines with a pencil. Your design will be transferred to the lino.

Sometimes I'll sketch in pencil right on the block, but this can get pretty messy. The dark, soft graphite line on the linoleum may smear, smudge, or be accidentally rubbed off. This smudging can be somewhat controlled by using a little workable fixative. Let's say, for instance, half of the graphite line drawing on the linoleum is finished, and you want to preserve it: simply give it a light spray of the workable fixative. Just remember that once it's sprayed the graphite line can't be erased.

Once your graphite line drawing is complete on the linoleum block and has been sprayed with the workable fixative, you're ready to begin cutting. Several types of lino cutters may be used. The lino knife, V-shaped gouge, large gouge, liner, and large liner are the most common. The shape of the tool point will give that shape in cutting. In general, the smaller point tools are for tight areas and detail. The wider point tools are for removing large areas, such as large, open background areas. These tools are very sharp; *all* cutting on the block should be done in the direction away from the body or other hand, which is holding the block in place on the table. This should prevent any unnecessary trips to the emergency room.

After the linoleum block is cut, both the workable fixative and the soft, dark graphite must be removed in order to strike an artist's proof or test print. First, you need a solvent for the workable fixative. The best one I've found is Bestine. I usually take everything outside for good ventilation; then I'll soak a cloth rag with the solvent and very gently rub the graphite off of the linoleum block. Chances are, all the fixative will be cleaned off with the solvent but not all the graphite. So step two is to gently wash the linoleum block surface with a rag and a mild soap-and-water solution to remove all of the graphite. Now you're ready to print. For that you'll need ink, a brayer, paper, and a large metal spoon.

Printing inks are either oil-base or water-soluble and are available in many colors. Water-soluble inks produce a rich, satiny finish, mix and tint easily, and are quick drying. Cleanup time is kept to a minimum. But in my opinion, the best prints are struck with oil-base ink. The water-base ink goes on a little too thick and has a tendency to plug up some of the finer cut lines, especially in a detailed lino cut. I use the water soluble ink only for striking proofs or printing short runs, because it cleans up much easier and faster. If you have to make small corrections or alterations on the lino block, it may take three or four separate test printings. You'll have to clean up the block between each test, so these first artist's proofs should be made with water-base ink. Because of its fast-drying characteristics, water-soluble ink should be thoroughly cleaned off of the brayer and lino after every four or five separate printings to prevent the ink from clogging up the finer line areas in the lino.

Oil-base inks will produce brilliant, clean, colorfast impressions on paper or cloth. The oil-base ink can be drastically thinned and still produce a dark, crisp image. Cleaning is done with kerosene, turpentine, or other similar solvents. Oil-base ink allows you plenty of working time, because it may take several days to thoroughly dry, depending on the amount of application and ink consistency. If you plan to make several prints in one sitting, I recommend this type of ink.

The brayer is a hand roller designed for inking printing blocks and plates; brayers are available with ei-

The percentage of dark areas in a linoleum print will often depend on the subject being pictured. Some artists will purposely leave as many dark areas as possible in a lino, using only highlights in these dark areas to show light and form. You can see the highlighting in the dark overcoat area of this print. I wanted to suggest that the man is well protected from the elements, so I kept detail within this dark area to a minimum.

Compare this with "Deep in Thought," page 114. In the latter, I eliminated most of the heavy, dark areas so they wouldn't compete with the finer detail areas. None of the unimportant background detail is pictured, so attention is focused only on the main detailed area, the woman's head.

Nor, Noreaster
Black, oil-base ink printed on plate-finish bristol board

ther hard or soft rubber. I prefer the soft, because I feel it gives me better ink coverage. Vary the directions of the brayer while applying the ink on the lino surface to be sure the entire surface is evenly covered.

The quality of your print will depend on the type of paper you use. You may choose to experiment with a rag or cotton-fiber paper, rice paper, newsprint, or whatever. I prefer plate-finish bristol board because this finish is a good-quality, hard surface that easily accepts both types of inks. Also, the paper is rugged because of its slight thickness and can take a beating when it is heavily burnished with the bowl of the spoon. Some of the edges and cut ridges of the lino can be sharp and may damage some types of paper. Water-based ink will further weaken the paper by moistening it. With this combination, the thinner types of paper such as newsprint or rice paper may tear if burnished too hard.

After you've applied the ink to the lino and placed the paper on the inked surface, use a large metal spoon to burnish the paper. Burnishing is done simply by rubbing the bottom of the spoon bowl over the paper. Be sure to burnish every part of the paper well.

When I produce a lino cut, I'll generally make only two or three proofs (in water-base ink) before running a small series of thirteen prints in oil-base ink. The most prints I've ever made of a single lino cut was three separate series of thirteen.

Deep in Thought
Linocut printed in black, oil base ink on plate-finish, 2 ply bristol board

As a general rule, the medium you choose and the way it's applied will influence the final look of the art. Let's compare the two linocuts "Deep in Thought" and "In the Corner of the Room" to prove this point.

First, "Deep in Thought" looks as if it were carefully planned and drawn out with a pencil; the end result of the cut and printed line systematically reflects this type of drawn pencil line. I don't think you'll be shocked to learn it was in fact drawn with a pencil directly on the linoleum block. On the other hand, I wanted "In the Corner of the Room" to be a strong graphic, an almost abstract representation of shape, form, and shadow. And I wanted the lines to look "brushed on" rather than "drawn," so I used a large (no. 12) watercolor brush with a watered-down solution of nonwaterproof India ink to sketch directly on the linoleum block. After the sketch was completed, I cut the block surface, then thoroughly washed it in a mild soap-and-water solution to remove any residual ink.

In the Corner of the Room
Black, water-based ink printed on plate-finish bristol board

115

Monotype

In this monotype the brushstrokes that were drawn on the glass are easily seen in the transferred print. One of the advantages of working with a brush is that you can mix the solvent and ink on the palette to the right consistency and thickness for each stroke you make.

Sleeping Model
Speedball black oil-base ink and brush drawn on glass, printed on 2 ply, plate-finish bristol board

A monotype is as the name implies "one print." Monotypes are made by inking or painting on a smooth, hard surface, then placing a piece of paper on the surface, thereby transferring the image to the paper and pulling a single print before the ink is dry. Odds are next to impossible that two monotypes will be identical, unlike linos, which produce the same print again and again. I've rarely seen monotypes commercially reproduced in ad campaigns—they fit mostly into the category of "fine art."

The surface you use for your monotype should be as smooth, clean, hard, and nonabsorbent as possible and as large or larger than your planned illustration. Some good surface materials would be a large sheet of metal, glass, Plexiglas, or hardwood. I use a sheet of glass because it's all of the above: it is an extremely hard and smooth surface, nonabsorbent and very easy to clean; also it's relatively inexpensive. A word of caution about the glass: the surface that the glass is set on should be clean and solid, like the floor or a strong table. If there is any small object, like a hairpin, under the glass when pressure is applied over the glass sheet while making or transferring the print to paper, that object can cause the glass to break—not a good thing when you are working with glass and your bare hands.

Printer's ink or slightly thinned oil paint works best for monotypes. Both come in a variety of colors. I use two types of palettes on which to spread my ink for the brayer. The first is a large sheet of aluminum foil which is securely taped down on a table top. This is inexpensive, strong, and instantly disposable. The second is an

extra sheet of glass which can sometimes get pretty messy to clean up. I prefer foil.

The best papers to use for monotypes are the smooth, plate-finished, lighter-weight types, namely, hot-press papers. You don't want to use a paper with a tooth or textured surface. The object of the monotype is to make the ink work for you, to show its created line, tone and texture and to use the paper to receive the inked image, to make this image permanent. Rough-toothed and textured paper surfaces would compete too much with the inked surface, and some areas and much of the line would be missed in the transfer.

Although this technique only results in one print at a time, monotypes can be produced in any of four ways and could almost be considered four techniques in one. The four monotype methods are (1) brush and ink; (2) brayer, ink, and tools; (3) reverse direct drawing (because the drawing is done on the reverse side of the paper, which is lying directly on the inked surface); and (4) direct monoprinting.

TYPE ONE: BRUSH AND INK

The first technique is to use ink and brush. Apply the ink directly on the glass surface. Darker areas in the drawing may be achieved by applying a heavier concentration of ink. Lighter areas will require more thinner or solvent mixed with the ink. As you are inking in the drawing, be aware that the ink on the foil palette will be used up, or the thinner will evaporate, or both. The brush will have to be dipped continually throughout the

This monotype was done with brush and ink, using the first technique described in the text. First I did a sketch in graphite, which I then placed under a large pane of glass to use as a guide in inking my monotype.

After the sketch and glass pane were in place, I squeezed ink into the center of a large piece of aluminum foil (the foil acts as a disposable palette). Then I dipped a clean no. 6 red sable watercolor brush into paint thinner and worked the wet brush and ink until the ink was diluted to a smooth, creamy consistency. I used the same brush to draw on the pane of glass with the ink.

For printing this monotype, the paper was placed over the inked surface of the glass when the brushwork was finished, and the bottom of the paper was taped in place. The print was struck using a tightly wadded rag to burnish the back of the sheet of paper with light pressure. Then the paper was carefully peeled off from the top down but left attached at the bottom with the tape. The print was analyzed and additional ink touchups were made with the brush, on the glass. The print was then carefully returned to the same position on the glass, and the wadded rag was used again to burnish and transfer the ink corrections onto the print.

Waiting for a Gentleman
Thinned black oil paint and brush drawn on glass, printed on Pentalic Paper for Pens

117

This monotype was done spontaneously without any planning or preconceived drawing or sketched ideas. I used the second technique described in the text, and the shapes and textures were created by the few tools I had on hand at the time.

First I placed a large sheet of white paper under the pane of glass to provide a neutral, clean background to build the monotype against. I used a soft rubber brayer to lay down the soft, slightly textured, dark gray background and foreground areas. Next, a single-edge razor blade was used to remove parts of the inked areas to create the negative shapes for the buildings. You can easily see where the blade was picked up and moved slightly to make the next line, and the buildup of ink on the blade fell off the blade to create and suggest the rocky coast in the center right and bottom right side of the illustration. Then, without wiping this blade off, I swung to the top of the monotype and made the vertical and horizontal lines in the background sky and the landscape depth lines, in the bottom left corner of the illustration. I then picked up the brayer and touched the inked side of it to the center left area for more graphic, horizontal landscape depth lines. Then, using only the end of the brayer, I created the cloud shapes in the sky area.

The phone rang, and I stopped to have a short conversation. While I was talking, I happened to pick up a wooden pencil and was using it as a drum stick, drumming on the table with the pink rubber eraser end. When the conversation was through, I unconsciously carried the pencil back with me to where I was working. Studying the monotype's progress, I decided it needed a different, graphic shape to add a little variety, and lo and behold, I had the tool right in my hand! I could use the pencil's eraser as a rubber stamp, so I began dipping the eraser into the ink and stamping it on the glass to produce the small, round, graphic shapes. I also wanted small, uniform rectangular shapes to represent windows—and a way to apply them, so as not to disturb the rest of the work already completed on the monotype. Eraser to the rescue. I cleaned the ink off the pencil eraser and cut sections off with my penknife. I made a few test stamps to get the rectangular proportions on the eraser just right, then began to add the windows in the buildings.

I taped the paper to the glass and followed the procedure described previously using a clean, wadded cloth rag with light pressure to burnish the back of the print. When I pulled the paper back to view it (it was still taped to the glass), I noticed the lower left corner hadn't transferred well. So I placed the print back in the same position on the glass and used my fingernail to burnish the paper. The darker, vertical rub marks in the lower left corner are the result of this, and it's obvious that different pressure was used. In a sense, this different pressure area improved the monotype because it balanced out the darker area above it in the sky. Thus, one of the lessons to be learned from this monotype example is to keep your burnishing pressure the same when working and reworking the ink transfer, unless you intentionally want to experiment.

Castle by the Ocean with Storm Clouds
Thinned oil paint on plate-finish, 2 ply bristol board

course of the drawing in the thinner to work the thicker ink on the foil palette into a diluted, thinner, workable consistency. Once the ink has been applied to the surface, it can be reworked with a variety of tools. Use a dry cloth or rag to erase or remove portions of the ink. Model the surface using objects of various shapes, such as a brush, single-edge razor blade, pencil eraser, a piece of inked burlap, wire mesh, or an old toothbrush. This is where your imagination can take over.

When the ink drawing is done to your satisfaction, it's time to pull the print. Carefully place a sheet of smooth paper over the inked surface. The trick at this point is to tape the bottom of the paper to the glass with plenty of masking tape. This will hold the paper in place while you burnish it, and keep it from slipping on the inked surface, creating a double image. Taping down your paper will also allow you to rework the print later, which is important because there is a good chance that not all of the ink will be transferred from the glass onto the paper.

Use the palm of your hand or a tightly wadded rag to apply light pressure to the paper, transferring the ink from the glass to the paper. When you've finished burnishing, do *not* remove the masking tape. Starting at the top, easily peel the print off the glass until the entire sheet of paper is up, but still taped at the bottom.

Since the paper is securely attached to the glass, the print can still be reworked at this stage. Minor additions or modifications can be made by rebrushing the ink on the glass surface.

Rework as much as you wish, but remember you can only add to it. Once the ink is transferred onto the paper, that is where it is going to stay; you cannot remove the ink from the paper unless you take rag soaked with thinner and rub the inked paper, and who knows what you'll end up with—probably a mess.

Once you've inked in the addition or corrections, the paper can be easily placed back in the exact, original position on the glass, and the new ink will be picked up and transferred onto the paper by reburnishing. When you are finished and satisfied with the

The monotype above employs the third technique described in the text. With the paper in place on the inked glass surface, I drew my design with a ballpoint pen, right. The tone areas in the brick background weren't intentional, but were caused by the weight of the paper resting on the inked glass. I created the other tones intentionally with slight fingertip pressure. Note that the print is a reverse of the drawing.

Gabriel
Thinned Speedball, black oil-base ink, drawn with a fine-nib ballpoint, printed on Pentalic Paper for Pens

Fish Print
*Thinned Speedball, black ink,
brushed directly on the fish and
printed on rice paper*

print, simply untape the paper from the glass. Remove all of the tape, and your print is complete.

Water-based ink will probably be completely dry in an hour, plus one or two extra hours to be safe for extra heavy ink applications. But allow at least two or three days for oil-based ink to dry completely.

TYPE TWO: BRAYER, INK, AND TOOLS

The second monotype technique variation is to use a brayer to completely cover the surface used for printing with an even, smooth coat of ink. Work this area by removing portions of the inked surface—again, your line and design will be affected by the tools you use. When the drawing is finished to your satisfaction, repeat the process described in Type One.

TYPE THREE: REVERSE DIRECT DRAWING

The third technique variation is similar to the second in preparation. Again, using the brayer, prepare the printing surface with a smooth, even coat of ink. Then place a clean, smooth piece of paper over the inked surface. The paper, once in place, shouldn't shift or move from side to side; secure it to the glass by taping down all four corners. Now you can draw directly on the paper surface; the pressure of the lines you draw will be picked up on the opposite inked side of the paper. Different drawing tools may be used to add a variety of line weights, but sharp,

pointed tools used mainly for drawing work best. Any pressure applied by a larger object (to achieve a type of texture) would only result in a self-defeating dark blob. Also, while drawing, be careful not to add any excess pressure on the paper surface by setting your hand or objects on it, or these will show up in your picture. When the drawing is complete, carefully remove the paper from the inked surface, and you'll have a monotype.

TYPE FOUR: DIRECT MONOPRINTING

The fourth monotype technique is a relief transfer method. *Relief printing* means the "raised" portion or surface area of an object, when inked, will transfer, or print. Any areas below this raised surface that have been removed or cut away aren't covered with ink and won't print. The linocut is a relief print, and the "Fish Print" on this page is a relief print. Fish printing is an ancient Chinese art.

BONUS TYPE

Just for fun, monoprints can be made from lino cuts. This is done by brushing (instead of using the brayer) colored oil paints on the lino cut and making a print of that. Some of the brushstrokes will be transferred onto the paper, and colors can bleed into each other. When this is printed in the lino line, it can be quite colorful and beautifully different. After the print has thoroughly dried, parts or areas of the print can be colored in, with either thinned oil paints or watercolors. I prefer thin oil washes, since these don't wrinkle and buckle as watercolors sometimes do.

To start a fish print, you'll obviously need a fish—be sure it has scales, some fish don't. My favorite brush is a one-inch, flat, watercolor brush. I used thinned, oil-based Speedball printer's ink to make this print. (I think oil-based inks produce the best results. Water-based inks dry too fast.)

The best paper (and the clue here is that it's an ancient Chinese art) is rice paper. The ancient Chinese didn't have mass-produced bond, newsprint, or bristol board, although in experiments, I've made some pretty successful fish prints on newsprint.

The trick to making a fish print lies in brushing on the ink. The ink must be thinned to a soft, creamy consistency, not too watery. All of the brushstrokes travel in one direction only: from the head backward over the scales to the tail.

After your fish is properly inked, pick up the paper and place it on top of the fish. Gently, mold the supple paper around the fish by applying very, very light pressure with your fingertips. When the fish's shape is completely covered, pick up and remove the paper. If the print isn't completely perfect, don't despair, it may take several tries to get the hang of it.

The print on the near right is a conventional print made from a linoleum block, taking care that the raised surface of the block (that made the print) was covered with a smooth, uniform coating of ink, which was evenly applied with a brayer.

Then the print was made in the conventional manner, by placing a sheet of paper on its inked surface and burnishing the paper to transfer the print. It doesn't make any difference how many prints you make from the block, all are going to look the same or have very slight differences.

This is not the case with the print on the far right. This same linoleum block can also be used to make one-of-a-kind prints, or monotypes such as this.

The carved image on the lino will stay the same, but instead of applying ink to the surface using a brayer,

Standard linoprint black oil-based ink printed on 2 ply, plate-finish bristol board

122

you use oil paints (different colors if you choose) and apply them to the surface of the lino with a brush. The oil paint colors may be used thick, right out of the tube, or greatly thinned, and colors can be premixed or literally mixed on the lino surface.

In some cases, the texture and direction of the brushstroke on the lino surface will be transferred onto the paper surface when the print is made. Each print may have a different color scheme and brushstrokes and texture; no two will look alike.

When the prints are thoroughly dried (allow three or four days), you can take it another step by shading or coloring in areas of the monotype with watercolors or very thinned, colored oil paint washes.

Monotype brushed-on colored oil paint for line print then lightly shaded with colors of oil paint washes. Painted on 2 ply, plate-finish bristol board

PART THREE

STYLES

Style is the visual end result of a technique or an application of art medium or a combination of mediums. Artists through the ages have tried to identify their style in such descriptive terms as "realistic," "surrealistic," "abstract," "nonobjective," etc. The first artists to consciously invent a style may have been labeled as "Cubists," "Impressionists," "Expressionists," or "Surrealists." Styles and famous artists' names are generally synonymous: Renoir and Monet (Impressionism), Seurat (Pointillism), Braque and Picasso (Cubism), or Dali (Surrealism). It's been said that you can become famous if you invent an art style.

Illustration style has changed dramatically since the turn of the century. In the early 1900s, a drawing or illustration had to look refined and labored over, and took, in some cases, months to complete. A sketch was called a "preliminary," and wasn't thought of as printable final art. Nowadays, more and more drawings are seen on television, in magazines, and in newspapers; sometimes these illustrations must be completed in a matter of hours to meet incredibly close publishing deadlines. A great variety in illustration has resulted from this spontaneous, fast-track life-style—you'll see everything from slick portraits and political cartoons to rough courtroom sketches, and interpretations of disaster-related news stories (floods, earthquakes, famine, terrorist activities) and sports happenings. An even different look has evolved with computer-generated graphics, which are being refined to an art.

It is also almost impossible to classify a piece of art—whether it's commercial art, text art, or fine art. I've seen commercial art and advertising displayed in the best art museums, and many fine art

pieces and paintings used for advertising. For example, take a famous painting by Renoir (any one), and you have a wonderful example of fine art. Now, let's throw a photo of it on a poster; is it then classified as poster art? . . . or advertising art? Now let's throw it on a greeting card and add the message "Hope you get well soon." What do we have then? Especially if the recipient didn't know of Renoir, would he or she call this a piece of fine art or commercial art? I don't know either!

Style as "Look"

In general, the visual style of the art will vary with a change in the application technique and the art mediums used; at times, the one may dictate how the other is used. There are different styles in *line* (dot-dash, saw blade, horizontal, etc.), *shading* (crosshatch, stipple, wash, etc.), *coloration* (monochromatics, etc.), and even the different *paper finishes* may lend themselves to creating different styles. Each medium is capable of rendering a variety of different styles, and when this medium is combined with another, the possibilities grow even larger. As you can see by my art, I don't rely on one style or one art medium to accomplish all of my illustration ideas. Variety in style ends boredom and offers much more to life. My only rule in art is to have fun and enjoy making art. (But on the practical side, artists with a variety of styles and techniques in their portfolios have a definite advantage over those with only one style.)

In the following gallery of illustrations, you'll see how dramatically style can vary, even when the same subject is rendered in the identical medium.

Dining Alone
Speedball Flicker lettering pen FB #6, waterproof India ink, drawn on Charrette bristol board #980

By now you have realized (if you already didn't know) that there are several variables in creating an illustration or drawing and changing just one of them will give a totally different look to the piece: the art medium or medium combinations, their technique in application, and of course, the paper texture or surface. The following four illustrations deal primarily with the same subject matter, that is, a table with a still-life arrangement, all viewed from slightly above, but the styles are totally different because of the way I combined the different art mediums, paper surfaces, and techniques. Secondary style differences are texture and minor differences in perspective.

"Still Life with Cake" shows an abstract style created by combining two separate perspectives—straight on and overhead. It was initially drawn with a brown marker on heavy watercolor paper. The rough texture of the paper was accentuated by the addition of pastel, which helps define and give form to the objects.

"Still Life with Table" is also inherently abstract, but its tight mechanical and linear style results from using a variety of line tones and widths. To create the straight mechanical lines you can use a ruler or metal straightedge, which tends to add a look of precision to the line.

Still Life with Cake
Sketched with a brown Chartpak AD Marker, then shaded with pastels, drawn on 140-lb. cold-press, Strathmore 500 watercolor paper

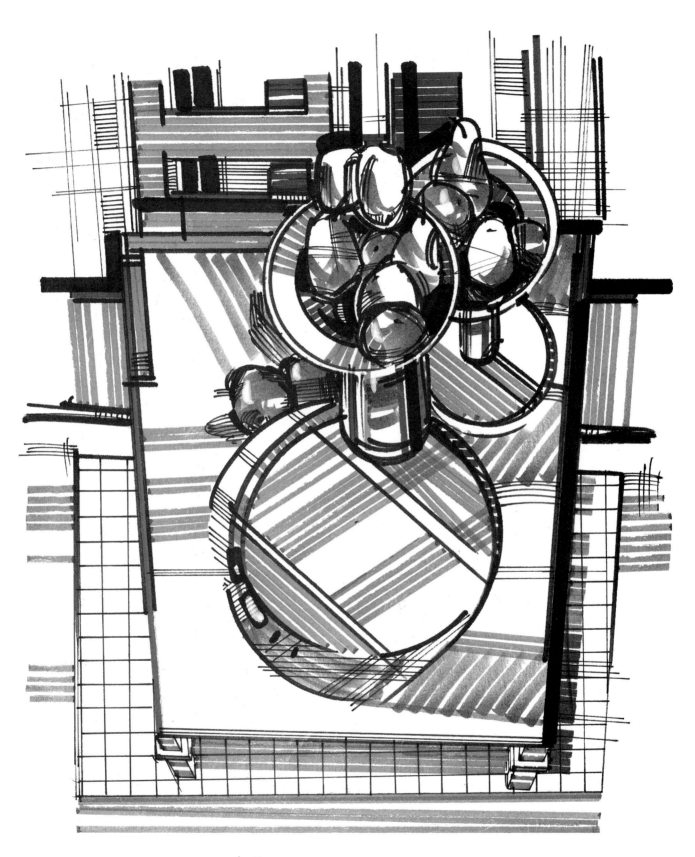

Still Life with Table
(fine lines, black) Pilot Razor
Point, (medium lines, black, gray,
and dark gray) Eberhard-Faber
Design Chisel Point, (heavy lines,
black) Eberhard-Faber Markette,
Strathmore drawing series 400 paper

Table with Fruit
*Waterproof India ink and brush
drawing with a waterproof India
ink wash, drawn on plate-finish,
Morilla artist's bristol pad*

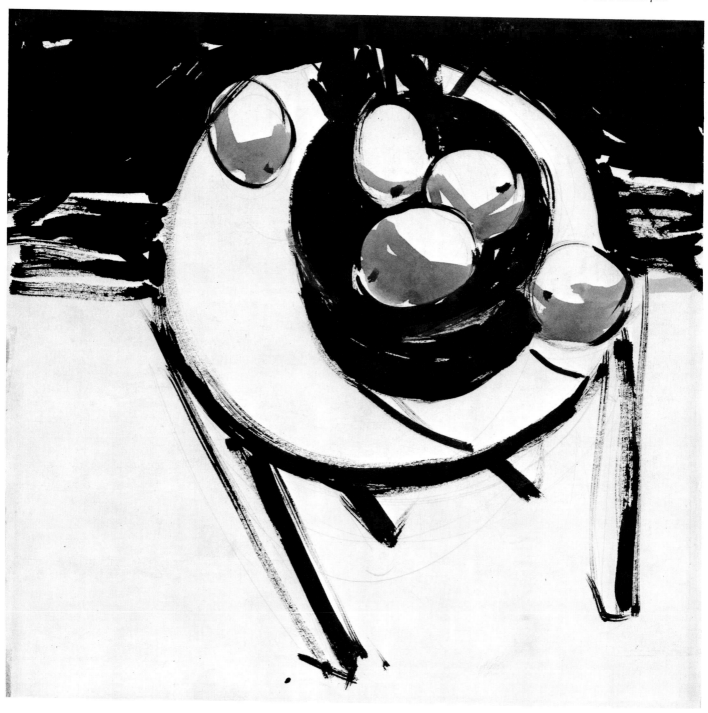

In the Corner of the Room
*Black, water-based ink printed on
plate-finish bristol board*

"Table with Fruit" was created with a brush and India ink. Both wet and dry brushstrokes appear, such as in the table legs, and are combined to add a freely drawn look and feeling to this illustration.

"In the Corner of the Room" was drawn with a brush on a linoleum block, then cut out and printed. This gave the brushed line a solid look. All of the brushstrokes were rounded off by the cutting tool. The style is more graphic than the three previous illustrations as a result of the printing process and careful inking of the linoleum block. The paper plays an important part, because ultrasmooth paper is necessary in order to allow all of the inked surfaces to print clearly. Any paper texture would be more of a hindrance than advantage when pulling a linocut.

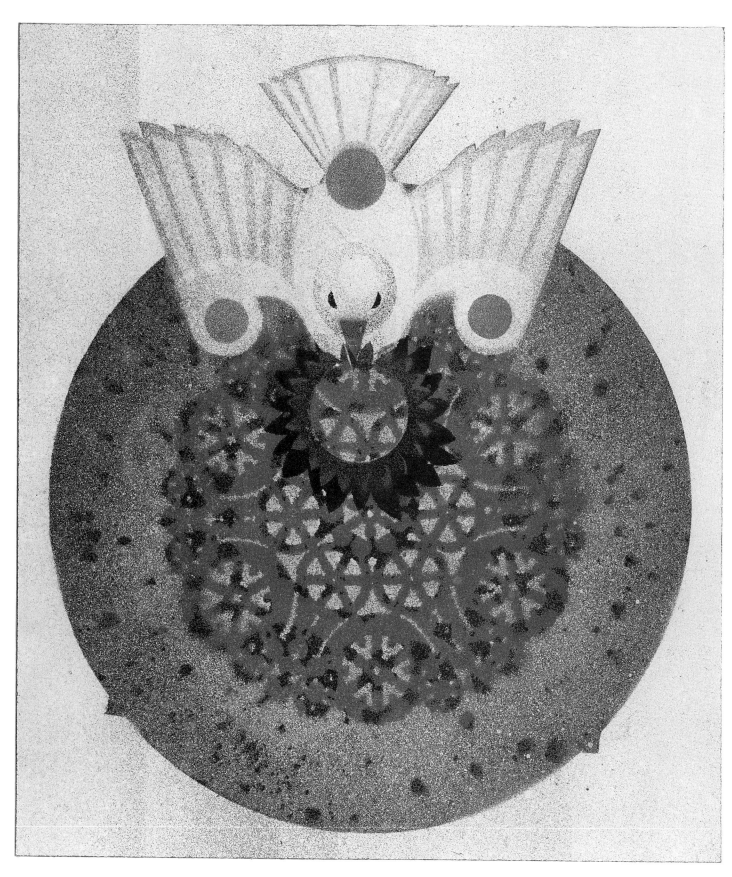

Dove of Peace #1
*Enamel spray paint and stencils,
on 2 ply plate-finish, bristol
board*

For "Dove of Peace #1," I used the aerosol technique to create a detailed and, since colors were used, very vivid style. This particular piece was carefully planned, its tones calculated and executed with stencils. There are no drawn lines whatsoever on this drawing, which gives it a tight look. The paper used is not of any importance in this picture. This piece was used as a holiday greeting card.

"Dove of Peace #2," a monotype, was drawn with a number of quick, varied brushstrokes, which are noticeable in its line and line texture. Unlike "Dove of Peace #1," this print is characterized by spontaneous, loose lines and results in a more "fine art" look. The paper you choose for this style is important; smooth, plate surface easily accepts and reflects the detail and characteristics of the brushed line. This print was a preliminary study for a holiday greeting card.

Dove of Peace #2
Thinned black oil paint and brush drawn on glass, printed on 2 ply plate-finish bristol board

As with the still lifes on pages 126-127, the figure drawings "Dining Alone," "Blueberry Picker," and "Woman on a Checkered Blanket" show the different styles or moods that are possible by varying medium, paper texture, perspective, and rhythm of line.

"Woman on a Checkered Blanket" features a high, almost aerial perspective. The dark surrounding tonal areas help to frame the loose line composition and emphasize the detailed central area, thus drawing the viewer's eye to it. This loose line style is spontaneous, and the drawn line does not look planned or labored.

"Dining Alone" is a quick gesture drawing that involves line only. This thin ink line, drawn with a lettering nib, is relatively uniform in thickness, and the drawing is meant to look flat, two-dimensional, and void of tone. The smooth surface of the paper easily accepts the line and does not hinder it by adding texture to it.

Woman on a Checkered Blanket ▲
(Thin lines) the edge of a 3.5 Niji Stylist Calligraphy pen. Combined (heavy lines) Eberhard-Faber Markette drawn on Charrette Concept 900 paper

Dining Alone ◄
Speedball Flicker lettering pen FB #6, waterproof India ink, drawn on Charrette bristol board #980

"Blueberry Picker" has a soft, subtle, spontaneous combination of drawn and scumbled lines. You can add tone by the use of the heavy, wide, scumbled graphite line, yet this style has a softness, which the graphite conveys. The rough texture of the paper is important because it allows the graphite line to show its characteristics.

Blueberry Picker
Graphite, Ebony pencil, drawn on rough newsprint

Line Styles

A line, as Webster's dictionary describes it, is "a thread-like marking, as with a pen, pencil, etc.; a stroke." A drawing or illustration may have different line weights (thicknesses), line sizes (lengths), and line characteristics. As you know, technique is a way of applying a medium or mediums to achieve a certain look or style. A change or addition in technique or application of line will often produce a different visual style.

In general, anything stylized has some distinctive characteristic, some subtle difference in line or form. To stress this point and visually explain, I've included a visual comparison—a set of three cartoon drawings that were drawn to produce different line styles. These styles are the *normal* line, the *dot-dash* line, the *irregular dot-dash* line, and the *saw-blade* line.

The primary reason for using different styles for a drawn line is simply to add more variety and to make the line more interesting. The more unusual the line, the more different the overall look of the drawing. These different line styles offer you some variety from the same old, humdrum, normal line.

NORMAL LINE

The normal line style is a simple drawn line that hasn't been varied by an additional technique. Everybody knows this one!

DOT-DASH LINE

The dot-dash line was developed primarily to add interest to an illustration. In this style, the illustration is composed of a series of random dots and dashes—unconnected lines, rather than a complete or continual line. This style lends itself well to cartoons and is more effective with a broad or heavy line.

For the dot-dash line it is best to use a black medium that will repro-

duce well; the darkness and boldness of India ink is very effective. A medium such as charcoal or graphite won't be as successful in rendering this line because of the soft edges and marks they make. However, other mediums can be combined with this style to produce tone variations. For these illustration samples I used ink alone to better show the line's character, but just about every other type of art medium you can think of can be combined with a dot-dash style (with the possible exception of opaque mediums such as oil paints, gouaches, and pastels). Mediums for all types of dilute wet and dry washes (such as watercolors, inks, dyes, acrylics, charcoal, or graphite), and other line combinations can be incorporated into a dot-dash line drawing. The possibilities are endless.

The tools used to produce dot-dash style should render a continuous line width; lettering nibs, technical pens, or felt-tip pens can all be successful. But probably the easiest way to draw the dot-dash line is with a technical pen, which will produce consistent line widths, even with the wider nibs such as #s 3.5, 4, 5, and 6. Use smooth, plate-finished papers to render the dot-dash line. Bristol board will best accept the India ink line.

This style is especially suited for spot illustrations and is best used in small doses. A large, full page illustration could be tedious for the viewer's eye to decipher because of the short disconnected line characteristics. When I use this style, I try not to complicate matters by showing a multitude of subjects, but use it to illustrate only one subject.

Also, an artistic use and selection of the dots and dashes is advisable. Don't repeat the same dot-dash selection over and over again. Staggering the selection of the dots and dashes and also adding a variety of line lengths will be visually more attractive.

IRREGULAR DOT-DASH LINE

This line is a variation on the dot-dash line in the sense that the line is also composed of a series of unconnected dots and longer dashes visually tied together to form a recognizable shape. This irregular, shaky line looks as if it were drawn by a very nervous person. This style also lends itself to cartooning but is best rendered in a thin, lighter-weight line, unlike the heavy, bold, dot-dash line. This type of light-weight, thin line needs the darkness and strength of India ink and can be well-executed with a #00 or #0 technical pen, a crow quill nib, a Pilot Razor Point felt-tip, or an extrafine lettering nib. Again, plate-finish bristol board is the paper of choice.

SAW-BLADE LINE

The saw-blade line, like the dot-dash line, was developed simply for illustration line interest. This style resembles the toothed edge of a saw blade. The distance of the acute angles of the line are equally spaced throughout the drawing. This distance between the acute angles may differ in different drawings; some may have less distance, and others may have more. This style works best with simple, less detailed drawings with a thinner line. Saw-blade style is, again, best suited to India ink or a Razor Point felt-tip pens. Technical pens (#s 0, 1, and 2) and drawing pens will also render a superb saw-blade line.

Normal Line

Dot-Dash Line

Irregular Dot-Dash Line

Saw-Blade Line

135

Broken Line

The broken line style is as its name implies: it has a slightly broken, old, nicked look.

The line can be easily drawn with a technical pen, a steel drawing pen, or a felt-tip pen, and is best produced in ink or black felt-tip. You either slowly build up the line thickness by a series of thinner lines, purposely leaving spaces and nicks in the line, or you draw the line completely and then re-work with Pro White and a brush to "paint" in the nicked parts. A third way to produce the line is to nick parts of the line off with the edge of a sharp razor blade. India ink used in a technical pen or lettering nib on a hard, heavy vellum paper will produce the best results. Again, other art mediums can be combined or added to produce tone variations.

Horizontal Line

The horizontal line style isn't as easy as it looks; it requires some planning. And the subject of the drawing should be kept simple for this style to be successful. The entire drawing—shape, form, and tone—is composed of horizontal line. The closer the lines parallel, the darker the tone in the area appears. If the drawing is to be reproduced or printed, it should be done as close to actual size as possible. This minimizes the chance (if the drawing has to be greatly reduced) of the horizontal lines filling or plugging in printing.

The technical pen is the only tool to use in producing this style because of its continual accuracy and quality ink line. Ink offers the best line reproduction in both the horizontal and

This line style's characteristic is the boldly drawn line that seems to be nicked or slightly broken as if with age. The broken line style adds a subtle difference and variety to what would be a normal line. This interesting line variation can be applied to spot as well as full-page illustration designs, and as you can see by the samples, *this technique produces a style that is well suited for graphic design.*

Samples of Broken Line Style
Waterproof India ink and technical pen, drawn on Charrette Concept 900 paper

vertical line styles (which follows). The ink line is more exact; the softer graphite or charcoal line won't be as sharp and crisp. But graphite is useful in the preliminary stages of rendering these styles, because it's best to begin by lightly penciling your design on paper.

When sketching out the drawing, the question to ask yourself is whether an area will be white or dark, that is, have line in it. Once you start thinking like this, the drawing will go much faster because you'll be able to plan out the white and linear areas and how they work with each other. To help myself when sketching out the drawing, I will often label the dark areas with a "D" as a paint-by-number board is labeled, so I can easily visualize these intended areas.

Once the drawing is complete, it's time to shift your thoughts to tonal values. Now you must decide *how* dark to make an area because the darkness will then dictate how close together the lines are. If you want to include black areas in this style or the vertical line style, there's absolutely no reason you shouldn't. (This may even create another style variation.) I didn't because I wanted to simply show the style with a range of closeness of lines and how they may visually relate to each other.

For the horizontal, straight lines, a T-square can be used; for freehand horizontal line, just draw the line, ink right over your sketch, then when the ink is thoroughly dry, erase the underlying graphite line.

To render the horizontal line illustration style shown here, you'll need a T-square and a drawing board or table. After you've planned and lightly sketched your drawing, tape it to the drawing board so that the subsequent horizontal lines will fall where you want them on the drawing. Use the T-square to apply the precise, straight lines, removing the T-square periodically to monitor your progress. Place your lines selectively to create positive and negative shapes, both of which are important to this style. To add tonality, vary the distance between the lines.

I employ tricks for balancing lights and darks in line illustration, such as in "Here's the Pitch." Notice *how both the background and the player's uniform are white. To show the shape of the uniform and still maintain a white outline, I added a few background lines to butt against the uniform, but I kept the lines spaced far enough apart so the overall background tonality is still light.*

After the drawing was complete, I used a kneaded eraser to remove the graphite outline of the drawing and added a little Pro White for touch-up.

Here's the Pitch
Horizontal line, drawn on Charrette Concept 900 paper, waterproof India ink and a #00 technical pen

The Two Detectives
Drawn on Charrette 900, heavy tracing vellum with waterproof India ink and technical pens.

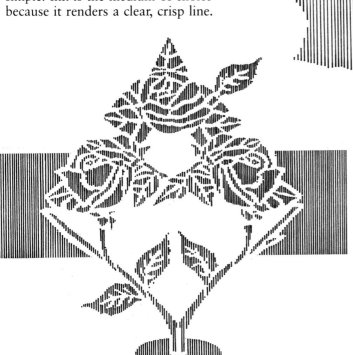

Vertical Line

This style is accomplished in the same manner as the horizontal line style, only in the opposite direction. All line in this style is vertically drawn. Again, shading and tones are achieved by the closeness of the lines to each other. The closer the line, the darker the area appears (and vice versa). As with the horizontal style, illustrations are most effective when they're kept simple. Ink is the medium of choice because it renders a clear, crisp line.

Rose Bush
India ink and #00 technical pen, drawn on heavy vellum paper

Once the design of "Rose Bush" was completed, instead of filling in the positive areas with solid black, I converted what would be the black areas into vertical line. Both the positive, vertical line areas and the negative, white areas were carefully planned to work together and complement each other in this graphic design.

Like "Rose Bush," "The Two Detectives" is made of the same type of close, equidistant line, but with one slight difference. Two different line thicknesses were used in the making of this drawing: a heavier line for the figures and a thinner line for the secondary

sign and shadow areas.

The heavier lines were drawn with a #2, and the thinner lines with a #0, technical pen nib. I used a T-square and medium-sized triangle to draw the vertical lines. This difference in the thickness of line helps to separate the figure shapes from the shadow areas; without this, the figure shapes would not be as well defined and would easily get lost in the shadows.

Note the importance and use of the white, negative areas in and around the drawing: they help tell the story of light, shape, and form.

Crosshatching

Crosshatching is the crisscrossing of line to build shading or add tonal values and texture to the drawing. Crosshatching is composed of lateral and diagonal lines, which will render a variety of tone darknesses. The four ways crosshatch lines can be formed are vertical, horizontal, and diagonal in both directions.

Be aware that the number of crosshatch directions does not determine the tonal darkness. As with the vertical and horizontal line styles, the tone or darkness of the crosshatched area is determined by the closeness of the lines to each other. Once again, the simple rule is, the closer the lines, the darker the tone; the farther apart the lines, the lighter the tone. Of course, when these lines are built up in layers, the tone will grow progressively

denser until eventually very dark tones or solid black is achieved.

The length, width, and shape of the crosshatched line may vary—straight, wavy, broken, or uneven lines can be drawn mechanically, using tools, or loosely rendered, by hand.

Folk Singer
Waterproof India ink and #00 technical pen with charcoal dry wash. Drawn on Charrette Concept 900, mounted on 2 ply plate-finish bristol board

In this illustration, crosshatching was used almost exclusively. This line technique is used throughout, from the shading, to the inner detail areas, and the sample was made to show that crosshatching can stand on its own as a style, created by the technique of the repetition of a series of built-up horizontal, vertical, and angular lines. The additional dry-wash tone was added for tone variation and to give the illustration visual boundaries on the upper part of the drawing. It was designed not to interfere or compete with the crosshatching.

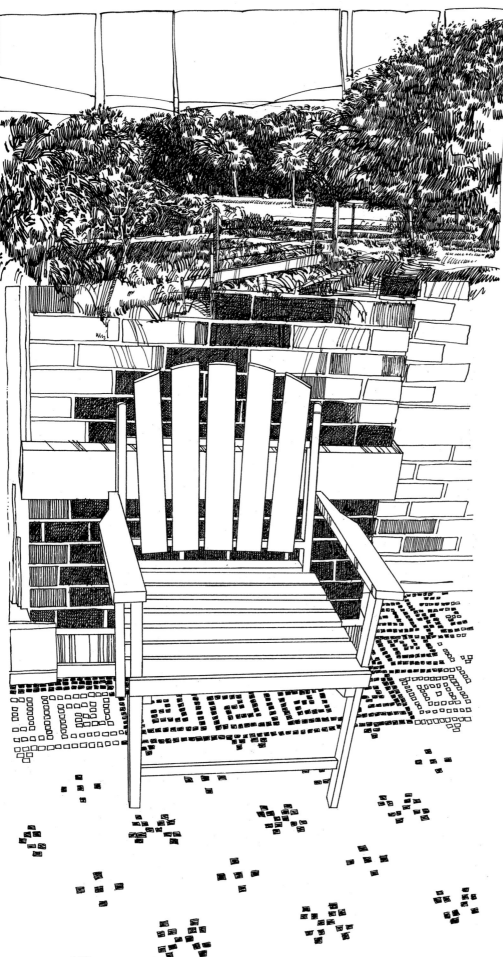

With some illustrations you'll find that a single technique is the key to pulling all the other elements in the piece together. Crosshatching was the finishing touch in "Chair for Dreaming" that made the concept for the piece work.

With ink, when you want straight lines—vertical, horizontal, or angular—use a technical pen and straightedge. Sure, it's easier to draw lines freehand, but they won't really be straight, and the look won't be the same. For instance, in this drawing, the chair is the focal point and probably the most important part of the drawing. Visually, the crisp straight lines in the chair create a new, clean, strong, and inviting look. If I'd drawn the chair freehand, the lines wouldn't have been straight, and the chair would have looked old and beat-up, unable to support any weight.

I began the piece by first drawing in the chair and brick wall. To this I wanted to add the surreal look as of a lingering dream of a tropical place, a daydream someone may have had while sitting in the chair. So I added the landscape in the background and made the sky and horizon open by simply drawing in suggestive horizontal lines for mountain *ranges.*

Next, to keep the chair from floating, I added a few random tile patterns on the floor, keeping the patterns open and free to balance the top of the illustration. The drawing then seemed to lack motion and to be top heavy; somehow I had to direct the eye from the chair and the outlined brick background upward into the landscape. I placed a sheet of tissue over the drawing and began experimenting by blackening in portions of the brick wall. I found that blackening some of the bricks around the chair not only pulled the eye upward into the landscape but also "popped" the chair out from the wall. But solid background bricks were too dark; they seemed to create small rectangular holes in the wall. My problem was solved when I found that linear crosshatching worked better.

Chair for Dreaming
#00 technical pen and waterproof India ink drawn on 2 ply plate-finish bristol board

This illustration uses crosshatching for depth and tone in limited areas only. These areas surround the most important parts of the illustration—the heads and football. First, the line drawing was lightly sketched with a graphite pencil. Then, using a #00 technical pen, I traced over the graphite line in India ink. When this was complete I had to decide where to add the crosshatching. Establishing the darkest area (and just how dark to make it) would determine the tone and depth for the rest of the illustration.

The first and darkest area to be crosshatched was the shadow, face, and helmet of the man carrying the ball. The smaller areas were done freehand, but for the larger areas a straightedge was used. The advantage of using a straightedge was control—it allowed me to control the distance between the crosshatch lines, keeping them equidistant and neat-

er than if I had done them freehand. I varied the direction of the crosshatch lines to add interest and variety to the illustration. In some of the tone areas, the crosshatching may be composed of one, two, and even three different directions. In areas of lighter tone, the lines are in only one or two directions, and are more widely spaced.

Run up the Middle
#00 technical pen, waterproof India ink, drawn on plate-finish, 2 ply bristol board

141

Hard-Edge Graphic

As its name suggests, this simplified, stylized graphic representation has an ultrahard edge. The bold, wider line always remains the same thickness throughout the drawing. These graphic designs are oversimplified, their bold lines making them strong enough to stand alone as design. Some of their uses include logo designs, decorative and spot designs, such as on matchbook covers, in advertising and display ads, game boards, and stickers.

A technical pen is best suited for this type of illustration because of its extreme accuracy in applying a crisp, smooth, continuous ink line. Other mediums such as charcoal or graphite won't render this sharp linear edge properly. I would also suggest you use tools to create this highly stylized line: a straightedge, circle guides, and varied degrees of ellipse templates. Needless to say, any drawing of this type with a ragged or uneven line edge would be unacceptable. Only a very hard, smooth, plate-finish paper is suited for this graphic approach.

Uniformity is the key word for the hard-edge graphic style. All lines should be uniform in line thickness. You can monitor your progress and line width accuracy: After you've drawn out the design in pencil, outline the broad lines with a technical pen and a straightedge. At this beginning stage, only outline the broad lines because if you make a mistake or make the line too broad it will be easier to remove a thin outline than a broad, solid line. After all the broad lines are completely outlined, check for accuracy in line width. Remember, all your line widths should be the same. Once you've checked the entire illustration and made sure the lines are all fine, it's time to fill in all the lines and finish the illustration. You'll need a keen eye to keep the line weights and widths the same throughout the entire drawing. You can use Pro White to correct line width after the fact. It can be brushed on, and when dry, the line can be redrawn over it. The problem may lie in the amount you have to use. In some cases, in order to completely "white out" the ink line, several coats of the

These illustrations are drawn in solid, hard-edge graphic line. The subject matter is designed and drawn in a simplified manner, which can easily be adapted to this strong, heavy, linear style. This style results in bold, independent designs.

Stylized samples of hard-edge graphics
Drawn with a #00 technical pen, then filled in. Waterproof India ink. Drawn on Pentalic Paper for Pens

#00 technical pen, waterproof India ink specially formulated for technical pens. All were drawn on Charrette Concept 900 paper

white may be needed, and three things may occur. First, you may succeed in overlaying a perfect ink line with the technical pen. Second, you may accidentally dig or chip away some of the Pro White with the thin point of the technical pen while trying to redraw the line. Third, as above, you may succeed in redrawing the perfect line, but in handling the paper (even at a later date), you may accidentally bend the paper, causing a piece of the Pro White to chip off. It may also lift off if a sheet of paper is accidentally slid across the top of the corrected surface. This has happened to me several times—it's the added risk you take. If I make a mistake in drawing the ink line, I automatically reach for my electric eraser, checking to make sure I'm using a green eraser with it. In small or tight areas in the drawing an erasing shield may be used.

Hard-Edge Graphic Variation

This is a hard-edge graphic style that combines two line thicknesses instead of just one. These line thicknesses consist of a heavy, bold line and a much thinner line. The bold line is designed to be used as a strong outline border to accentuate and highlight the most important parts of the design; the thinner lines create detail within the heavier line. Once the thicknesses of both the bold and thin lines in this style have been established, they should remain the same throughout the entire drawing. This style offers a little more visual variety than the regular hard-edge graphic.

This illustration style uses a hard-edge graphic line in two thicknesses. A T-square and straightedge were used throughout, with the exception of the background palm trees. Notice that the line quality may differ slightly in certain areas and is not offensive to the eye, but the line thicknesses will always remain the same. "Hollywood" was done with pressure-sensitive lettering, which I added for the final *touch. This type of illustration is accepted and used commercially.*

Hollywood
Drawn with a #1 (.45mm) technical pen and waterproof India ink on Pentalic Paper for Pens

This is a variation of the hard-edge line graphic style in the sense that a loosely drawn parquet pattern has been added. This pattern can be used as a design element (large-sized patterns) or as a tone (smaller-sized patterns) and can be informal (freehand line) or formal (lines precisely measured in relation to each other and drawn with a T-square and straightedge). This particular design could be used commercially for all types of playing card paraphernalia.

Nothing Up My Sleeve
Drawn with a #1 (.45mm) technical pen and waterproof India ink on Pentalic Paper for Pens

Mechanical style uses a very formal, precise, accurate line that is formed with the aid of tools and a technical pen. Many professions will use this type of line, from designers, engineers, and drafters to graphic artists. This style takes time, patience, and much practice to keep the line quality consistent, clean, and accurate.

Sample of Mechanical Style
Waterproof India ink and technical pen, drawn on Pentalic Paper for Pens

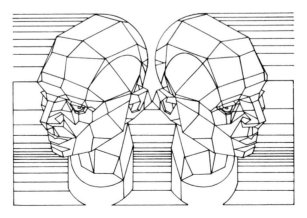

Hard-Edge Graphic with Parquet Pattern

This variation can be combined with the other styles in the hard-edge graphic family. The difference lies in the tone patterns, which are made up of a repeated alternating parquet pattern. Again, line widths should be consistent, although they can range from fine to bold. This style is well suited to decorative spot illustrations.

Mechanical Style

This style is a form of drafting, and is usually rendered in a technical manner with the help of tools such as the straightedge, compass, T-square, triangle, ellipse guides, French curves, and circle templates. Thus, anything drawn in a loose, freehand fashion doesn't resemble the mechanical style. Mechanical pencils and technical pens are most often used. India ink in a technical pen renders a precise line, its width consistent throughout the entire drawing. Smooth, plate-finished papers are best for producing the mechanical line style.

The illustrations in this section show only a few of the mechanical line style's many possibilities. The visual variety is almost endless with the introduction of different line styles. However, the mechanical style is mostly used commercially—much of the tight board work in product illustration, such as product renderings, blue prints, assembly procedures, drafting and exploded views, is done in this style.

These illustration samples show a clean line that employs different types of tools, such as circle and ellipse templates, straight-edge and T-square, and different sized and shaped french curves to create this linear, mechanical style.

The first sample, top left, shows a combination of line styles; the tones in the printer were achieved by adding the crosshatch style.

The second sample, top right, combines line, simplified silhouette shapes, and different tonal background and stylized shadow.

The third, bottom left, combines grayed toned lines of the background computer with black lines to highlight and bring out the foreground printer. The computer is enhanced with stippled tones.

The fourth, bottom right, uses line and the silhouette of a man. Tones are created with graphite dry washes.

Stylized samples of hard-edge graphics
Drawn with a #1 technical pen, then filled in. Waterproof India ink, drawn on Charrette Concept 900 paper

Silhouette

A silhouette is a dark shadow area that is first outlined and then completely filled in. Silhouetting is one of the oldest art forms and can be traced as far back as the ancient Greeks, whose pottery featured figures and objects drawn or painted with highlight lines. In the eighteenth and nineteenth centuries, silhouettes took on another form—cut black paper mounted against a contrasting sheet of paper that was then framed. These silhouettes were snipped with small sharp scissors and were most often done as portraits. In the twentieth century, silhouettes took on still another form: they were spray painted on glass panes and placed against different background colors and motifs that could easily be changed. For example, a silhouette spray painting of two lovers embracing, with a background painting or photo of a moonlit, Pacific cove makes a romantic picture, but change the photo to a large African tiger in an attacking position, and the embracing couple are in real trouble!

Any recognizable figure, object, or shape can be made into a silhouette. Profiles are generally used; silhouettes should have sharp, cleanly drawn edges. The best mediums to use in rendering silhouettes are India ink and linoleum prints. All types of smooth, plate-finished papers work well with this style.

Once my pencil drawing and planning stages for a silhouette are completed on paper, I'll outline all the borders of the silhouette with #1 technical pen. When this is done, I will again go over and "beef up" this outline line with the same #1 techni-

Samples of silhouette-style Waterproof India ink and technical pen, drawn on Pentalic Paper for Pens

The silhouette is a simplified dark design, profile, or shadow shape, with little or no inner detail. Both of the animal silhouette samples deal with just black-and-white areas, no intermediate tones. "Deer" is a solid type, and descriptive, negative, white spaces have been left out. These descriptive areas were used in "Goat" and are seen as white lines surrounding the back, legs, and hoofs of the goat in the foreground. These lines are meant not to highlight, but to separate one object from another. Please note, these white lines could easily be filled in, and the picture would still nicely succeed as a solid silhouette.

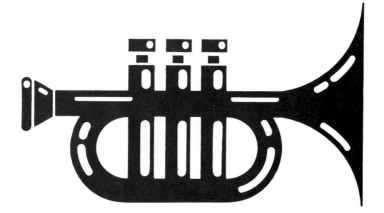

cal pen. Next, to fill in the outlined areas, I will change over to a thicker, heavier technical pen nib size, like a #3, which minimizes the effort in filling in the areas to be solid black.

I use a technical pen mainly because of its built-in ink supply. You may choose to use a drawing pen if you don't mind continually dipping it into the ink.

Graphic Silhouette with Rounded Line Highlights

The descriptive title establishes this as a silhouette with inner highlights, which add to the visual demarcation of the object. Essentially, these highlights are large designed white shapes which are usually overstated and rounded at the ends. These highlights may add interest, design, shape, or contour, inside what would normally be a solidly filled silhouette. The approach is graphic, which suggests and simplifies the detail into basic, simplified, hard-edge, stylized forms and shapes.

The technical pen and ink are the best tools to create the ultracrisp, smooth-line edges for this style. A template makes it easy to render the highlights. On larger drawings, a fine-line technical pen (a #00) can be used to outline the graphic; then either a wider technical pen (a #3), or a small brush can be used to fill in the larger dark areas of the silhouette.

I use this style mainly for spot illustrations or small drawings. As with the hard-edge graphic style, small doses of this strong style are best.

This style is simply the addition of hard-edged highlight shapes to the silhouette style. In the illustration "Trumpet" the highlight shapes help direct the eye around the trumpet's form and add contour to the design. The illustration "Evolution in Generations" shows a variety of different highlight shapes and uses, which not only add to the overall design but also help to create graphic differences in the three beetles. I use a template to create the sharp highlight forms and also Pro White to clean up any irregularities in the shapes. I suggest using a smooth, plate-finish paper along with India ink to produce the clean, sharp edge characteristic of this style.

Samples of graphic silhouette with rounded line highlight style
Waterproof India ink and technical pen, drawn on 2 ply plate-finish bristol board

Wood Grain

This style of illustration resembles a piece of wood—the wood grain composes the flat solid shapes of the design. I keep several different prints and rubbings of different wood grains to help me in rendering this style.

First, I draw the outline shape of my design on tissue paper, then place this over a wood grain print. This allows me to position the drawing in the most interesting area on the print. Then I trace the grain pattern using pen and ink on the paper. If I want a tighter grain, I will simply fill in between the lines with additional lines. This way I can control the distance and tightness of the lines in the drawing.

The drawn line of the wood grain can be rendered in different ways: crosshatched, stippled, normal line, or any combination of these.

The wood grain style in the drawing above is used only in the design areas of deep shadow. Because it is so highly stylized, it almost borders on a wavy, horizontal line style. I use India ink and a technical pen to create the line in this style, primarily so I wouldn't have to constantly dip a steel drawing pen in ink.

Wooden Dime
Wood grain style. India ink and #1 technical pen drawn on Charrette Concept 900 heavy vellum and mounted on plate-finish 2 ply bristol board

The drawing, right, combines the silhouette and wood grain styles for a humorous effect. Notice how this grain differs from that in "Wooden Dime." You might want to keep rubbings of interesting wood grains on hand. Before you trace your wood grain, position and plan your drawing carefully: I intentionally minimized detail in the head and neck of the rooster to maintain a strong silhouette in these areas.

Rooster
Drawn with a #0 (.35mm) technical pen and waterproof India ink on Pentalic Paper for Pens

Cartoon

These caricatures or animated drawings are familiar to everyone. Cartoonists can often be recognized by their own specific style. These recognizable caricatures differ in line and style and may serve different purposes. There are political cartoons, comic strips, cartoon magazines, and humorous spot cartoons for magazines to name a few different types.

In cartooning, I guess you could say "anything goes" when it comes to mixing different types of line, mediums, and papers. Cartoons can employ combinations of all mediums, such as color, ink, paint, graphite, charcoal, or felt-tips. All types of imaginative lines and line thicknesses and all types of tones and shading will successfully work in rendering cartoons.

The term "cartoon" is like a large umbrella—many of the styles illustrated in Part Three could be classified as cartoon styles. Depending on the individual artist's interpretation of the meaning, the dot-dash, broken line, normal line, and even some of the graphic types could be called cartoons.

This cartoon is rendered in a heavy, regular line, and no intermediate tones were used simply because they weren't needed to express the feeling that "his time was up."

Second Thoughts
Drawn with a #3.5 (1.0mm) technical pen and waterproof India ink on Charrette Concept 900 paper

Two cartoon illustration samples
*#3 technical pen and waterproof
India ink drawn on Pentalic
Paper for Pens*

The cartoon "Cat" was meant to be a light, humorous magazine ad, and was not meant to be a realistic feline portrait. What cat wouldn't sleep easier and take comfort in knowing he is insured and protected by his insurance policy? The uncluttered, bold, simple line easily tells its story and is conveyed in a quick glance, the eye doesn't have to labor over the drawing to get its message.

The cartoon of the "Planes" uses the over-sized, round bumble bee shape that aerodynamically couldn't fly. The planes were drawn to appear to be made out of plastic and blown up like balloons. The line is drawn simply, with a little more detail than in "Cat," and the shadow areas are rendered using a crosshatched line technique.